Development Leads · Crystal Frasier and
Owen K.C. Stephens
Authors · Alexander Augunas, David N. Ross, and
Owen K.C. Stephens
Cover Artist · Kiki Moch Rizky
Interior Artists · Tawny Fritzinger,
Kiri Østergaard Leonard, and Simul

Editor-in-Chief · F. Wesley Schneider
Creative Director · James Jacobs
Executive Editor · James L. Sutter
Senior Developer · Rob McCreary
Pathfinder Society Lead Developer · John Compton
Developers · Adam Daigle, Crystal Frasier,
Amanda Hamon Kunz, Mark Moreland,
Owen K.C. Stephens, and Linda Zayas-Palmer
Senior Editors · Judy Bauer and Christopher Carey
Editors · Jason Keeley and Josh Vogt
Lead Designer · Jason Bulmahn
Designers · Logan Bonner, Stephen Radney-MacFarland,
and Mark Seifter

Managing Art Director · Sarah E. Robinson
Art Director · Sonja Morris
Senior Graphic Designer · Adam Vick
Graphic Designer · Emily Crowell

Publisher · Erik Mona
Paizo CEO · Lisa Stevens
Chief Operations Officer · Jeffrey Alvarez
Director of Sales · Pierce Watters
Sales Associate · Cosmo Eisele
Marketing Director · Jenny Bendel
Vice President of Finance · Christopher Self
Staff Accountant · Ashley Kaprielian
Data Entry Clerk · B. Scott Keim
Chief Technical Officer · Vic Wertz
Software Development Manager · Cort Odekirk
Senior Software Developer · Gary Teter
Project Manager · Jessica Price
Organized Play Coordinator · Tonya Woldridge
Adventure Card Game Designer · Tanis O'Connor

Community Team · Liz Courts and Chris Lambertz
Customer Service Team · Sharaya Copas,
Katina Davis, Sara Marie Teter, and Diego Valdez
Warehouse Team · Will Chase, Mika Hawkins,
Heather Payne, Jeff Strand, and Kevin Underwood
Website Team · Christopher Anthony, William Ellis,
Lissa Guillet, Julie Iaccarino, and Erik Keith

ON THE COVER

What was supposed to be quick and clandestine reconnaissance quickly turns violent in this colorful illustration by artist Kiki Moch Rizky.

TABLE OF CONTENTS

REFERENCE

This Pathfinder Player Companion refers to several other Pathfinder Roleplaying Game products and uses the following abbreviations. These books are not required to make use of this Player Companion. Readers interested in references to Pathfinder RPG hardcovers can find the complete rules from these books available for free online at **paizo.com/prd**.

Advanced Class Guide	ACG	*Ultimate Combat*	UC
Advanced Player's Guide	APG	*Ultimate Intrigue*	UI
Ultimate Campaign	UCA	*Ultimate Magic*	UM

Paizo Inc.
7120 185th Ave NE, Ste 120
Redmond, WA 98052-0577

paizo.com

Introduction

From the elusive Lion Blades of Taldor to the fierce law enforcement agents of Absalom's Starwatch, spies operate in every corner of Golarion. Even groups primarily concerned with faith, magic, and fighting must look to their secrets; be it Desna's faithful in Nidal, Mendevian templars, or the Tempest-Sun mages of Nantambu, every organization has some need for spycraft.

This book explores many of the skills, resources, and backgrounds of great spies and spy-catchers across the world of Golarion. A wide array of backgrounds reward spies for maintaining connections with invaluable allies and protecting their own secret pasts from rival agents who might exploit their relationships or regrets. Spy organizations and their rivals also offer a variety of tools, spells, and items for their spies, including unique options for vigilantes, the new class introduced in *Pathfinder RPG Ultimate Intrigue*.

WHAT MAKES A SPY?

Spies operate in every walk of life. What unites them is their understanding that secrets are power. A spy seeks out other's secrets while preventing them from learning useful information about herself. She takes pains to observe whatever potentially valuable intelligence she can, preferably without being noticed, or manipulates events to ensure certain outcomes. Clues about future exploration opportunities in recently opened Osirian tombs, rumors of new experiments in Alkenstar that might yield better

or cheaper firearms, the habits of an Aspis Consortium merchant who has a strange tendency to stumble into dangerous places—all these are things any adventurer might observe, but a spy takes note of each and watches for opportunities to exploit the information or sell it to someone who will find it useful.

Most of the time, a spy outwardly appears to be uninterested in gathering intelligence in her daily life. To avoid detection, she must invest a great amount of effort in cultivating a career or lifestyle that isn't obviously connected to her true goals. In most cases, spies rarely just collect information. They also find opportunities to exploit vulnerabilities they discover. Strategies for capitalizing on information vary widely from spy to spy, but all appreciate the leverage superior intelligence provides and all take care to prevent others from gaining it over them. Most undertake missions with obvious motives so that none think to look for hidden objectives (or consider plotting to stop the spy from achieving hers).

Of course, the traditional image of the Lion Blade swashbuckler delivering vital intelligence for his nation's safety after a dramatic escape from an exploding wizard's study has some basis in truth. Deep-cover spies and information brokers often take on the appearance of dashing duelists, court advisors, or noble knights in shining armor so they can move about the circles of power undetected. These spies take on these personas based on having a similar actual background, after years of training with a spy organization, or even by simply paying careful attention to their surroundings and relying on sheer skill and force of personality.

SPIES ON GOLARION

Spy organizations generally have a set of interconnected goals. They serve to keep their leaders abreast of any new or relevant information related to their leaders' goals and interests, while protecting information that might be of use to opposing organizations. They engage in secret missions that must either not be connected back to their patrons (often for political reasons), or that are effective only if they aren't common knowledge (such as sabotage efforts and operations designed to misdirect foes). They also support and reward those who assist them (knowingly or unknowingly), such as adventurers and other spies.

The most common sorts of spy groups serve governments or those who directly oppose governments. The Twilight Talons of Andoran, the Risen Guard of Osirion, and the Lion Blades of Taldor are but a few of the groups that keep governments aware of opportunities and threats. The Silent Enforcers of Nidal, the Pure Legion of Rahadoum, and the church of Razmir all seek out any clues they can find to track down revolutionaries or those who engage in illegal worship. Conversely, rebels and freedom fighters hunt for weaknesses they can exploit and potential allies who also defy their governments in secret. These range from the Heralds of Summer's Return in Irrisen to the Bright Lions of Mzali in the Mwangi Expanse. All must fend off mundane questioning and tests of loyalty alongside divinations and other magical methods of oppression from their governments.

Others spies serve private organizations, such as information brokers and churches. Sczarni families notoriously dig up secrets they can use for blackmail, confidence games, or stealing even more valuable prizes. The church of Calistria often serves as a neutral information dealer to motivate and facilitate revenge plots both great and small. The faith of Asmodeus maintains countless active spies whose reports eventually reach the faith's mortal leader Aspexia Rugatonn in Cheliax.

Instead of serving organizations, some spies are freelancers or lone wolves, using the techniques of spycraft for their own profit or personal goals. This might mean discovering a map to a lost Thassilonian ruin and beating the original discoverer to the riches within, uncovering how a rival in the Ruby Phoenix Tournament has cheated and turning the tables, or learning the schedule of a shipment of slaves out of Okeno to arrange an ambush with support from the Gray Corsairs. Independent spies often were originally trained by an organization, which might not appreciate a spy who takes her training and resources without continuing to serve. Independent spies tend to have old debts or hostile former employers who would love nothing more than to find and punish them.

RULES INDEX

The following new rules options in this Pathfinder Player Companion are located on the indicated pages, alongside several other options found throughout this book.

Spells are organized by theme in each section of the book, as noted under Other Rules Options below. Each set of spells covers a range of classes and spell levels, providing new options for a wide variety of classes.

Hidden Backgrounds

Everyone has a past, and most spies take great care to keep some part of their pasts secret. When gathering valuable information, they learn to protect knowledge about their own interests and weaknesses. The following backgrounds, drawbacks, and traits are built using the rules in *Pathfinder RPG Ultimate Campaign*, and reference many traits and drawbacks from that book as well as new options presented beginning on page 6.

ESPIONAGE ORIGINS

Once you select the sort of spy your character is from the options below (agent, mole, saboteur, or spymaster), you can either choose a background from the corresponding table or roll randomly on the table to determine it. Most of the selected backgrounds grant access to either one trait or two traits and a drawback. As normal, taking a drawback entitles the character to a free trait. If you choose a background that has two traits and a drawback and you take both traits as well as the drawback, your third trait can be any sort of trait

appropriate to your character—you can even choose a trait of the same type as one of the background's traits (which is normally prohibited). This benefit assumes that your GM allots each player character the option of either two traits or three traits and one drawback. Work with your GM to determine the benefit if your game grants characters more or fewer traits or drawbacks.

AGENT

Agents operate in the field, collecting information at every opportunity. Agents train in Perception and Sense Motive to detect anything unusual as they go about their adventures. All classes can be agents, but this is most commonly a role for druids, inquisitors[APG], investigators[ACG], and rangers.

d%	Result
1–15	**Calistrian Initiate**: You worked in a temple of Calistria, where you learned to listen with great care when others are at their most relaxed. You gain access to the Calistrian courtesan and charming traits, as well as the lonely drawback.
16–30	**Consecrated Confidante**: You stumbled upon a dangerous secret once while counseling a member of your faith, and ever since have listened all the more closely to those who cross paths with you. You gain access to the divine confidante trait.
31–45	**Galtan Collaborator**: In order to stay alive in the chaotic nation of Galt, you quickly learned you had to condemn someone to the Gray Gardeners' guillotines at least occasionally to keep attention off of you. You gain access to the bully trait and the guilty fraud drawback.
46–60	**Patriotic Vigilance**: You believe in your nation's ideals and have earned respect for your ability to notice threats against it. You gain access to the official ties trait.
61–75	**Rootless Warrior**: Whether you're a Varisian wanderer, a Kellid barbarian, or some other adventurer, you have learned to keep moving to avoid difficult questions while profiting from selling the information you stumble upon to interested parties. You gain access to the friend in every town and reactionary traits, as well as the secret shame drawback.
76–100	**Itinerant Scholar**: You found travel to be the best way to get exposure to a wide array of magical techniques, including closely guarded ones that might be dangerous to share. You gain access to the secret scrolls trait.

MOLE

Moles position themselves to infiltrate locations and organizations under false pretenses. Most are skilled at

Bluff, Disguise, and Stealth. Practice with enchantments, illusions, or transmutations is also quite invaluable to them. Bards, rogues, slayers[ACG], and wizards are popular classes for moles.

d%	Result
1–15	**Lovesick Warden**: Before you even reached adulthood, you joined the border patrol to watch enemy armies posturing near Kalabuto or Nirmathas, and fell in love with someone from the other side. You gain access to the frontier-forged and tactician traits, as well as the lovesick drawback.
16–30	**Chelish Informant**: Whether raised in a free nation or under Chelish authority, you dismiss fanciful idealism and wish to share in the amazing power and wealth of Cheliax's rulers under whatever identity is most useful. You gain access to the Chelish sympathizer trait.
31–45	**Kitharodian Actor**: The Kitharodian Academy taught you to see real intrigue like a performance you could master with enough practice and sacrifice. You gain access to the mentored and youthful infiltrator traits, as well as the empty mask drawback.
46–60	**Twilight Impersonator**: You once glimpsed a Twilight Talon surprise and attack an oppressor while disguised as an innocuous professional, and were inspired to develop the skills of a spy even though Andoran could offer you no official support. You gain access to the ordinary and surprise weapon traits, as well as the stateless agent drawback.
61–75	**Wolf in Sheep's Clothing**: You were groomed from a young age (perhaps by drow, geniekin, or gillmen) to live among a foreign people as one of them in order to help conquer or undermine them. You gain access to the deep cover trait.
76–100	**Double Agent**: Your government trained you in the ways of revolutionaries and dissidents so you could move among them and goad them into revealing themselves. You gain access to the official ties and vigilant battler traits, as well as the paranoid drawback.

SABOTEUR

Saboteurs specialize in exploiting the information they glean from fellow spies or their own observations, striking foes when and how it will hurt them the most, preferably without exposing themselves. Saboteurs favor Craft, Disable Device, and Knowledge skills. The most popular classes for saboteurs are alchemists[APG], fighters, rogues, and wizards.

d%	Result
1–20	**Avenger**: You were orphaned and raised as a vengeance-seeker by a vigilante or a secretive organization such as the church of Calistria. You gain access to the grief-filled and youthful infiltrator traits, as well as the attached drawback.
21–40	**Criminal Enforcer**: As a young tough in the territory of a criminal organization, you demonstrated a talent

for exploiting enemies' vulnerabilities. You gain access to the criminal and dirty fighter traits, as well as the infamous drawback.

d%	Result
41–60	**Impure Thinker**: Raised in Touvette, Nidal, Rahadoum, or another nation that suppressed your religion, you seek out any way you can to undermine the authorities without drawing attention to yourself. You gain access to the hidden faith trait.
61–80	**Ninja Training**: You were raised by a ninja clan of Minkai to use stealth as both a tool and a weapon to gain glory and honor for yourself or your clan. You gain access to the criminal roots trait.
81–100	**Quantum Problem-Solver**: You witnessed a devastating magical accident in Nex, possibly engineered by the Invisible Blades, and realized how easy it would be to eliminate anyone undetected in similar fashion. You gain access to the dangerously curious and mercenary traits, as well as the magical klutz drawback.

SPYMASTER

Spymasters collect and analyze data from subordinate spies. Effective spymasters maintain covert contact with their spies, train in Bluff and Sense Motive, and are often spellcasters. Arcanists[ACG], inquisitors[APG], oracles[APG], skalds[ACG], and sorcerers tend to make effective spymasters.

d%	Result
1–15	**Bellflower Sown**: You stumbled into a Bellflower Network group moving slaves out of Cheliax and saved the group with a quick improvisation. You gain access to the slave runner trait.
16–30	**Child of the Resistance**: You were raised among dissenters in an oppressed nation such as Galt, Irrisen, or Mzali, who found your youthful idealism inspiring in the face of tyranny. You gain access to the dedicated defender and natural-born leader traits.
31–45	**Corrupt Official**: You were selected at a young age to serve your community in a public role by drawing secretly upon connections and information derived from political favors and Drumish or Taldan money. You gain access to the heir to corruption trait.
46–60	**Reputable Business**: You earned a position of respect in your community by passing the tests of the esteemed Prophets of Kalistrade, and can easily spend time talking to almost anyone without question. You gain access to the Kalistocratic prophecy trait.
61–75	**Spiritual Guide**: Your faith encourages you to counsel anyone who prays to your deity (whether or not he has chosen her as his patron), making you the perfect choice to coordinate agents serving your faith or an allied organization. You gain access to the persuasive insight trait.
76–100	**Military Strategist**: You were implicitly trusted by soldiers or officers impressed by your strategic instincts. You gain access to the Wily Warrior story feat (page 17).

ESPIONAGE TRAITS

Because the young are so often underestimated, spies often find their first opportunities for espionage come even before adulthood. Full rules for traits can be found on page 326 of *Pathfinder RPG Advanced Player's Guide*.

Chelish Sympathizer (Social): You feed intelligence to the Thrice-Damned House of Thrune for your own gain or ideological reasons and are given valuable clues gathered by other Chelish spies in exchange. Once per month while in an Inner Sea region settlement of at least 2,000 people, you can call upon these connections to gain an edge in a verbal duel (*Pathfinder RPG Ultimate Intrigue* 176) or gain a +2 bonus on one Bluff, Diplomacy, or Intimidate check.

Criminal Roots (Social): Your family has long operated outside the law. You gain a +2 trait bonus on Diplomacy checks to influence criminals and on Intimidate checks to influence law-abiding citizens, but take a –2 penalty on Diplomacy checks to influence law-abiding citizens. Diplomacy or Intimidate (your choice) is a class skill for you.

Deep Cover (Social): You have lived a double life since your youth, perhaps to avoid persecution for your true identity or in service to an enemy of the people or group associated with your cover identity. You can always take 10 on Bluff and Disguise checks to assume and maintain your cover identity. Bluff or Disguise (your choice) is a class skill for you.

Divine Confidante (Faith): You were inspired with the reverence offered by worshipers to priests and other spiritual leaders, so you assisted them. You gain a +3 trait bonus on Sense Motive checks to get hunches about those who discuss matters of faith, mythology, morality, religion, or the Outer Planes with you. Sense Motive is a class skill for you.

Hidden Faith (Faith): You were raised in a religion forbidden by your government, and draw strength from your hidden faith. You gain a +1 trait bonus on saving throws against the divine spells of creatures that worship a god other than your own.

Kalistocratic Prophecy (Faith): You were raised under the Prophecies of Kalistrade, and were inspired to seize upon an untapped business opportunity. Up to once per week, when you work to advance this opportunity with at least 1 day of effort, you can attempt an appropriate Profession check to earn money or gain capital using the downtime rules (*Ultimate Campaign* 76) with a +2 trait bonus. In the event of a failed check, your opportunity is discovered by rivals and you cannot employ this trait for 1 month while you look for a new opportunity.

Official Ties (Social): You maintain a friendship with one or more figures of authority. You have minor sway with one of these figures if your game uses individual influence (*Ultimate Intrigue* 102). You gain a +2 trait bonus on Diplomacy checks to influence people in positions of authority aware of your contact and who have an attitude of no worse than indifferent toward the government the contact represents. You also take a –2 penalty on Diplomacy checks to influence criminals and agents of opposing governments, if those characters are aware of your association with authorities. If you lose your contact, you lose the benefits of this trait for 1 month, after which you can make a new contact.

Persuasive Insight (Faith): You were converted to your faith or taught to bargain with spirits for magic by a figure of inspiring insight who taught you to use keen observation in all dealings. You can use your Wisdom modifier in place of your Charisma modifier on Diplomacy checks to ask favors or gain influence (*Ultimate Intrigue* 102). During a verbal duel (*Ultimate Intrigue* 176), you can use your Wisdom modifier in place of your Charisma modifier when using tactics you assigned to Diplomacy or Wisdom-based skills.

Secret Scrolls (Magic): You were inducted into a secret magical tradition such as the Esoteric Order of the Palatine Eye. You can cast *read magic* once per day as a spell-like ability, and gain a +1 trait bonus on Use Magic Device checks to activate scrolls you cannot normally use.

Slave Runner (Social): You witnessed or were party to the rescue of a halfling from Chelish slavery by the Bellflower Network or Eagle Knights. Once per day when attempting to directly free a slave, you gain a +2 trait bonus on your choice of an Acrobatics check, an Escape Artist check, a Stealth check, or a skill check attempted as part of a heist (*Ultimate Intrigue* 118) or pursuit (*Ultimate Intrigue* 142).

Wary Eye (Combat): You know that you could be exposed at any time. Even your closest friends could someday become enemies, and so you have trained yourself to never be surprised by a betrayal. At the beginning of combat, before initiative checks are revealed, you can select one opponent you are aware of to be the subject of this trait. If you succeed at a Wisdom check opposed by the subject's initiative check, you are not considered flat-footed against this subject for this combat, even if you normally would be. You can use this trait in a surprise round, even if you cannot otherwise act that round.

Youthful Infiltrator (Combat): You were trained from a young age to ambush the enemies of your order or organization, which makes you hard to trust for most outside your organization if they learn your affiliation. You gain a +1 trait bonus on attack rolls against flat-footed foes, as long as they have not seen you make an attack with this bonus before.

ESPIONAGE DRAWBACKS

Many spies push themselves to excel all the more to compensate for vulnerabilities in their backgrounds or secrets they fear being discovered. Full rules for drawbacks can be found on page 64 of *Ultimate Campaign*.

Betrayed: You were reported to a dangerous authority such as the Gray Gardeners of Galt, the high inquisitors of Cheliax, or the Council of Mwanyisa of Mzali, and narrowly escaped death. You second-guess your instincts constantly, leaving you never sure whether or not to trust someone and endangered if you encounter that group's agents again. You can roll twice and take the lower result on Sense Motive checks to get hunches. You cannot reroll this result, even if you have another ability that would normally allow you to do so.

Empty Mask: You have spent so long hiding your true identity to escape political enemies that you have lost much of your sense of self. You take a –1 penalty on Will saving throws against compulsions. This penalty increases to –2 against foes who know your true identity.

Guilty Fraud: You received something through trickery that you did not deserve, and your guilt for the misdeed distracts you from dangers around you. You take a –4 penalty on Bluff checks against creatures with an attitude toward you of indifferent or better.

Infamous: You were publicly linked, truthfully or not, to a crime of significant infamy. You draw attention wherever you go and risk imprisonment or worse in the jurisdiction where the crime was committed. You and your apparent allies take a –4 penalty on Diplomacy checks to interact with law-abiding citizens (except enemies of the authority that accused you).

Information Overload: You have had access to thousands of spy reports, many of which turned out to be based on faulty deductions or even intentionally false stories spread by opposed spy groups. At this point, you have been exposed to false knowledge as much as accurate information, and you can't always remember which is which. You take a –2 penalty on all Knowledge checks, and if you fail a Knowledge check by 5 or more, you can recall information that is diametrically opposed to the truth.

Lonely: You are far too easily convinced of the friendly intentions of others. You take a –2 penalty on Sense Motive checks and on Perception checks to see through disguises, and on saving throws against charm spells and spell-like abilities.

Magical Klutz: You were born in a place with a plethora of strangely interacting magic, such as Geb, the Mana Wastes, or Nex, and magic is dangerously eager to surge into action around you. You roll twice and take the lower result on Use Magic Device checks to activate items blindly and on Reflex saving throws against effects produced by magic items.

Occult Bargain: You draw magical power from a source, such as a mysterious eidolon, shame-filled phantom, or First World patron, who insists that its identity remains secret. You take a –1 penalty on concentration checks, and you must invoke the entity's name by word or text each day or be unable to regain spell slots that day. You must be able to cast 0-level and 1st-level spells as a class feature to select this drawback.

Righteous Indignation: You have difficulty controlling your temper after living in inhuman conditions in Cheliax, Geb, Irrisen, Katapesh, or Qadira. Whenever a foe provokes an attack of opportunity from you, you must take it unless you succeed at a Will save against a DC equal to 10 + your level. You take a –1 penalty on Will saving throws against spells with the emotion[UM] descriptor that do not also have the fear descriptor.

Secret Shame: You have a terrible fear of the public at large, a group, or an important person (such as your order of knights, your liege lord, your family, or your lover) learning a shameful truth about you. You take a –1 penalty on saving throws against fear effects, and the DC of any Intimidate check to demoralize you is reduced by 1. If you would normally be immune to fear, you do not take these penalties, but instead lose your immunity to fear (regardless of its source).

Too Many Secrets: You've told too many lies, and made up too many cover stories, and now even you can't keep it all straight. The lies have become reality to you, which makes it difficult to think of a new convincing lie. You hesitate at crucial moments when trying to fool those around you, and likely shouldn't be in the field at all anymore. You take a –2 penalty on Bluff checks and saving throws against illusions.

Vainglory: You compulsively seek recognition for your deeds, making it hard to act with subtlety. You take a –1 penalty on Bluff, Disguise, and Stealth checks, and the save DC of any illusion you create is 1 lower than normal.

Dangerous Ploys

Spies are well aware that unusual situations call for unusual skill techniques.

SKILL OPTIONS

Skills are a flexible and important part of the Pathfinder Roleplaying Game. Of course, it is impossible to list every way a skill might be used, which can sometimes leave a GM with little guidance on how difficult an unusual skill check should be. GMs might make the following skill uses available to any character who specializes in clandestine operations. Each description below expands the options for one or more skills. Checks using these new options work as normal for the relevant skill, except as noted.

COERCION (INTIMIDATE)

Sometimes you need to cow someone into submission for more than just a few hours.

Check: By spending more time threatening or harassing a target, you can attempt to force a creature to act friendly toward you for 1d6 hours + 1 hour for every 5 points by which you exceed the DC. If you succeed at such a check against the same target at least once per week for 1d6 weeks (without ever failing any Intimidate checks against the target during that time), the duration of the coercion increases to 2d8 days. Coercion is overt, not subtle, and in most cases using coercion against a creature is an evil act.

A coerced target acts as though friendly toward you even when you aren't around, but the aid offered remains grudging at best. The target's true attitude is hostile, and if the target believes it can take an action to hinder you that can't be traced back to it, it's likely to take such opportunities. Creatures attempting to enlist its aid against you can often do so by convincing the target they are able to protect it from your wrath, using the normal Diplomacy rules.

Action: Coercing a target into acting friendly for hours takes 1d4 × 10 minutes. Coercing a target into acting friendly for days requires you to successfully use coercion at least once per week for 1d6 weeks without failing any Intimidate checks against the target during that time.

Try Again: You can't attempt long-term coercion against the same target again for 1 week.

INCONSPICUOUS ACTION (BLUFF)

You can avoid drawing attention to yourself when performing conspicuous actions such as picking up an object in a museum where handling the exhibits is frowned upon but not a matter of grave concern, or closely studying someone across a room at a party.

Check: Your Bluff check is opposed by observers' Sense Motive checks. You can't attempt the check if your very presence is suspicious (which you could prevent by altering your appearance with the Disguise skill).

Action: You attempt the Bluff check as part of performing the action you wish to render inconspicuous. Normally, you must take twice as long as normal to perform the action in order to make it inconspicuous. A standard action becomes a full-round action completed just before the start of your next turn and a free, immediate, move, or swift action becomes a standard action.

INTENTIONAL MISHAP (USE MAGIC DEVICE)

You can intentionally cause a magic item to produce a mishap.

Check: You can cause a magic item to have an intentional magic mishap, as if you had attempted to activate it blindly and failed by 10 or more. The DC to produce an intentional mishap is 30. If you succeed, you have some control over the mishap. The item deals 2d6 points of damage to any one creature or object that the item could have targeted if activated normally. You can attempt to aim it, but if you select an invalid target, you take the damage instead. If you

Recall Intrigues (Knowledge)

Task	Knowledge Skill	DC
Identify a class feature from a class that grants arcane or psychic spells	Arcana	10 + class level when feature is granted*
Identify a class feature from a class with access to the druid or ranger spell list	Nature	10 + class level when feature is granted*
Identify a class feature from another class that grants divine spells	Religion	10 + class level when feature is granted*
Identify a class feature from any other class	Local	10 + class level when feature is granted*
Identify a combat feat being used	Local	10 + character's level
Identify a metamagic feat being used	Arcana	10 + character's level
Identify a teamwork feat being used	Nobility	10 + character's level
Identify any other feat being used	Local	15 + character's level

* Add 10 to the DC if the class is a prestige class.

fail the check by 9 or less, you create a normal mishap you do not control. If you fail by 10 or more, nothing happens.

Action: Attempting to create a mishap is like activating an item blindly, and requires a standard action during which you try out magic words or other appropriate actions.

Palm Weapon (Sleight of Hand)

You can draw a light weapon without anyone noticing.

Check: A successful DC 20 Sleight of Hand check allows you to unobtrusively draw a weapon or other object no larger or longer than a light weapon (which includes potions, but not wands or alchemist bombs). Observers can notice you drawing the item as normal with opposed Perception checks. Creatures carefully observing you gain a +4 bonus on this Perception check.

Recall Intrigues (Knowledge)

You can identify feats and the class features of various classes with successful Knowledge checks when you observe the feats or class features being used.

Check: You can attempt a skill check to identify a feat or class feature when you observe it in use, similar to how Spellcraft can be used to identify a spell. The feat or class feature must have some observable effect in order for you to attempt the Knowledge check. For example, you can't see the internal determination of Iron Will, so this ability can't identify that feat. In general, if a feat or class feature creates a noticeable effect (such as the extra attack from using Cleave) or has a variable modifier a character must choose to use (such as Arcane Strike, Combat Expertise, or Enlarge Spell), it can be identified. If it creates a static bonus (such as Dodge or Lightning Reflexes), there's no telltale sign to give it away.

The Knowledge skill required to identify a feat or class feature varies depending on the type of feat or class feature to be identified and is outlined in the Recall Intrigues (Knowledge) table above, along with the DCs of such skill checks.

OBSERVATION FEAT

Spies are often trained to gain vital information through skilled observations. This can be done with feats such as

Measure Foe^{UI}, Play to the Crowd^{UI}, Sense Assumptions^{UI}, and Sense Relationships^{UI}. The following feat is designed to assist in making similar trained observations, and is available to any character who meets the prerequisites.

Sense Loyalties

You can quickly sense a target's relationship to some specific god, patron, or government, and use that knowledge to manipulate them.

Prerequisites: Knowledge (nobility) 1 rank, Knowledge (religion) 1 rank.

Benefit: After 1 hour or more of interaction, you can attempt a DC 20 Sense Motive check to get a hunch in order to intuit what god, government, leader, or patron a creature is loyal to or worships. You must understand the language the creature is speaking, and if it's of a different type than you, you take a −5 penalty on the check. If the creature is attempting to conceal its loyalties, it attempts a Bluff check. If the result of the Bluff check is higher than 20, that result becomes the DC of your Sense Motive check. On a success, you learn whether the creature has a patron god, a witch patron, or a government to which it is strongly loyal. You can attempt to name one specific god, patron, or government for every 2 ranks you have in Sense Motive by introducing them into the conversation as subjects, as noted below.

You can use this ability only if you observe the creature in an environment where loyalty to a god, government, leader, or patron is being discussed. If this isn't already occurring, you can introduce the topic, but doing so may expose your interest. In this case, the creature you are observing and any other creatures able to hear you bring up the topic of loyalty to a god, government, leader, or patron can attempt Sense Motive checks (opposed by a Bluff check from you, which the GM rolls in secret). On a success, the creature realizes you are interested in determining the observed creature's specific loyalty. If you are attempting to determine whether the observed creature's loyalty is to a specific god, government, or leader as noted above, creatures who succeed at the Sense Motive check are aware of the specific god, government, leader, or patron about which you are interesting in learning.

Concealed Loyalties

To a spy, loyalty is the most precious commodity. Loyalty to an organization has its costs in secrecy and lost independence, but is typically rewarded with loyalty to the agent—and benefits such as useful assets to carry out both official missions and the spies' private exploits. You can represent your status within and favors owed by an organization via reputation and Fame (*Pathfinder RPG Ultimate Campaign* 180), with the organization as your sphere of influence. The following rules elaborate on a special use of this system by which organizations reward members for completing specific secret missions.

The organizations mentioned below can be used with prestige awards and related rules found in other sources as mentioned in their descriptions.

SECRET MISSIONS

Secret missions are a specialized form of award purchased with Prestige Points (*Ultimate Campaign* 182) that grants an opportunity to gain further Fame by achieving a specific goal. Like story feats (*Ultimate Campaign* 66), secret missions have prerequisites, an initial benefit, a goal, and a completion award (see below). Upon accepting a secret mission (which follows the same rules as awards), you immediately gain the initial benefit and a goal. If you complete the goal, you also receive the completion award.

Prerequisites: A mission's prerequisites usually include a minimum Fame score, representing how much an organization must trust you before it is willing to delegate the mission to you. The organization must fall within your Sphere of Influence (*Ultimate Campaign* 181) for your Fame to apply. If a mission costs Prestige Points, that cost must be paid in full the first time you undertake the mission; if you undertake it again after completing or failing it previously, you pay only 1 PP.

Benefit: You gain this initial benefit as soon as you accept a mission. You do not lose it even if you fail the mission.

Goal: This is the goal you must achieve to gain the mission's completion award. Often, you must meet the goal within a limited amount of time, which represents how long the organization can afford to wait before reassigning the mission to another agent.

Completion Award: This is the benefit you gain when you complete a mission's goal.

Failure: A secret mission has specific parameters, so it can be conclusively failed. A failed mission continues granting its benefit, but you do not gain its completion award.

Repeat Missions: Unless noted otherwise, a mission can be attempted again after 1 month, whether your previous attempt was successful or not. The new mission must have a new and more challenging target than the last. The initial benefit and completion award do not stack with those gained from previous missions, but might be applied to other categories or groups, if appropriate.

Secrecy: As the name implies, secret missions are generally pursued in strict confidence. Although close allies may be permitted to know the basics of the mission, most organizations frown upon sharing mission parameters beyond a strict need-to-know basis. If a mission's goal is clearly to be secretly achieved, then public knowledge (or discovery by enemy organizations) automatically results in failure. Beyond this, the organization does not care how a mission is accomplished, and a spymaster able to trick others into doing her dirty work is rewarded just as lavishly as an agent who takes care of things herself.

PUBLIC ORGANIZATION MISSIONS

The following public organizations need agents to discretely handle affairs that, if exposed, would negatively affect their public images or leave them vulnerable to their enemies.

BUREAU OF CRIERS SECRET MISSIONS

The Bureau of Criers (*Pathfinder Campaign Setting: Occult Mysteries* 20) investigates unexplained happenings across Golarion to further the research of its mysterious leaders.

INFILTRATE A MAJOR ORGANIZATION

You are granted identities of recently kidnapped or slain members of a major organization to assume in order to gain entrance to this organization.

Prerequisites: Fame 15, 5 PP.

Benefit: You gain a +2 circumstance bonus on Disguise checks to assume the identity of a member of the chosen organization and on Knowledge (local) checks to know about the group's history and contacts.

Goal: Within 1 week, learn of a new plan to be carried out by the group you infiltrated and thwart it.

Completion Award: Your Fame score increases by 2, and you gain a +4 bonus on Bluff checks to tell a lie corroborating an ally's lie.

CALISTRIAN SECRET MISSIONS

Calistrian churches and organizations like the Wasp Queens of Kyonin further the ideals of trickery, revenge, and pleasure.

BROKER

You are given the name of a foe to thwart through trade.

Prerequisites: Fame 15, 2 PP.

Benefit: Once per month, you can treat a settlement as being one size larger when determining whether you can buy or sell a single item. You must choose to use this ability prior to seeking a buyer or seller.

Goal: Within 1 month, successfully sell a cursed item to a challenging foe without being identified.

Completion Award: Your Fame score increases by 2.

PERSONAL REVENGE

You are supplied with a target who has wronged an ally.

Prerequisites: Fame 5, 1 PP.

Benefit: Once per day, you can roll twice and take the better result on a Diplomacy check to gather information about an individual.

Goal: Within 1 month, deliver revenge against a target unaware you are looking for her, overcoming a challenging foe in the process.

Completion Award: Your Fame score increases by 1.

CHELISH SECRET MISSIONS

Cheliax secretly sponsors spies all across the Inner Sea region to undermine rivals like Andoran and Taldor and to catch Chelish citizens acting against Thrune or the church of Asmodeus.

INFILTRATION

You are given gear and a cover identity to blend in to a governmental or military organization in Absalom, Andoran, Galt, Isger, Korvosa, Molthune, Nidal, Rahadoum, Sargava, or Taldor.

Prerequisites: Fame 15, 1 PP.

Benefit: You gain a +4 circumstance bonus on Disguise checks to impersonate members of that organization. Your cover identity is plausible but difficult to check, and includes documents that can be detected as forgeries only with a successful DC 25 Linguistics check.

Goal: Within 1 month, apprehend or slay a violator of Chelish law hiding outside of Cheliax, evading or overcoming a challenging foe in the process.

Completion Award: Your Fame score increases by 2, and you are granted free spellcasting services worth a total of 50 gp × your Fame score by a cleric of Asmodeus, though you must provide any expensive material components or foci required.

EAGLE KNIGHT SECRET MISSIONS

The Eagle Knights undertake missions not officially endorsed by their democratic nation of Andoran, most notably sending Gray Corsairs to liberate slave vessels, Steel Falcons to help political defectors, and Twilight Talons to monitor and undermine oppressors everywhere.

ESCORT DEFECTORS

You are provided with falsified documents that grant you permission to enter a specific enemy group's territory without being subject to close official scrutiny, and must safely bring back at least one defector.

Prerequisites: Fame 10, 1 PP.

Benefit: You can attempt Survival checks to cover your tracks and those of up to five other creatures without slowing down.

Goal: Within 2 weeks, escort at least one defector to Andoran without being followed.

Completion Award: Your Fame score increases by 1, and you gain the ability to spend 1 PP to enter the defector's home nation with documents that can be detected as forgeries only with a successful DC 25 Linguistics check.

GUERRILLA STRIKE

You are tasked with assaulting your foes quickly and quietly.

Prerequisites: Fame 20, 1 PP.

Benefit: Once per day as a standard action, you can allow up to five allies within 30 feet to take 10 on Stealth checks even if stress and distraction would normally prevent them from doing so.

Goal: Within 1 month, spring a surprise attack upon an oppressive military, such as that of Belkzen, Cheliax, Korvosa, Molthune, Nidal, or Razmiran that thwarts a challenging group of foes.

Completion Award: Your Fame increases by 2, and you can purchase a single weapon at a 10% discount.

LIBERTINE PIRACY

You must intercept a ship suspected of carrying slaves or slavers.

Prerequisite: 1 PP.

Benefit: You are given passage on a Gray Corsair vessel.

Goal: Within 1 month, defeat slavers who constitute a challenging encounter or liberate a number of slaves equal to your character level.

Completion Award: Your Fame score increases by 1, and you can purchase one sea vessel at a 10% discount.

PURGE CORRUPTION

You must cut out the rot within Andoran.

Prerequisites: Fame 15, 3 PP.

Benefit: Once per month, you gain a +5 bonus on a Diplomacy check to gather information about a political scandal or rumored spy.

Goal: Within 1 month, expose an enemy spy or a corrupt politician operating in Andoran.

Completion Award: Your Fame increases by 2, and you can obtain a single free casting of *atonement* for its lesser effect at a future date.

SHIELDMARSHAL SECRET MISSIONS

The Shieldmarshals protect the Grand Duchy of Alkenstar from crime, and hunt down those who conspire to undermine it or its monopoly on the manufacture of firearms. In quieter times, they also act as traveling protectors for communities struggling to reclaim the Mana Wastes.

Industrial Counterintelligence

You are alerted that certain Alkenstar crafting techniques have been stolen or offered for sale on the black market.

Prerequisite: 2 PP.

Benefit: You gain a +2 bonus on Sense Motive checks to get a hunch or use a feat that requires a successful Sense Motive check.

Goal: Within 1 week, get back the stolen intelligence and prevent its sale.

Completion Award: Your Fame increases by 1, and you can purchase one firearm or enhance one existing firearm.

Undermine Competition

New technology discovered in Numeria could threaten Alkenstar's position if it were reproduced.

Prerequisite: 2 PP.

Benefit: Knowledge (engineering) becomes a class skill for you; if it is already a class skill, you gain a +1 bonus on checks with that skill.

Goal: Within 1 month, buy or steal the item from Numeria without being stopped by the Technic League.

Completion Award: Your Fame increases by 3.

SECRET ORGANIZATION MISSIONS

The following organizations must keep most of their operations secret. Additionally, those with public fronts or proxies must ensure that trouble with those cannot be traced to any entity behind them.

Bellflower Network Secret Missions

The Bellflower Network uses a clandestine web of safe houses and secret trails all to smuggle halfling slaves to freedom outside Cheliax.

Front-Room Contact

You are trained to learn information from minimal conversation, as befits one who appears to be a servant.

Prerequisite: 1 PP.

Benefit: You can use your Sense Motive modifier in place of your Diplomacy modifier on Diplomacy checks to gather information.

Goal: Without the use of magic, influence an aristocrat in a slave-trading nation to have an attitude of friendly or better toward you.

Completion Award: Your Fame increases by 1, and you can call upon the contact once per month to attempt a Diplomacy check to gather information anywhere the aristocrat has influence.

Plant a Garden

You are directed to obtain a magic item that could be of use to the Bellflower Network.

Prerequisite: 3 PP.

Benefit: Appraise and Spellcraft become class skills for you; if either is already a class skill, you instead gain a +1 bonus on all checks with that skill.

Goal: Secure the magic item (worth at least 500 gp × your Fame) without being caught or tracked.

Completion Award: Your Fame score increases by 1, and a bard sympathetic to the Bellflowers grants you free spellcasting services worth a total of 50 gp × your Fame score, though you must provide any expensive material components or foci.

Brotherhood of Silence Secret Missions

The Brotherhood of Silence is the largest thieves' guild in the Inner Sea region. Its members are known as thugs and blackmailers and suspected of pulling the strings of many important government officials.

Quiet Enforcer

You are given the name and location of an individual who knows too much about the Brotherhood.

Prerequisites: Fame 10, 4 PP.

Benefit: If you move no more than a single 5-foot step each round, you apply only half your armor check penalty for armor you wear to Stealth checks.

Goal: Within 1 week, eliminate the target or seize all the target's evidence on the Brotherhood.

Completion Award: You can move up to half your speed and still not apply armor check penalties on Stealth checks, and your Fame score increases by 1.

Silence Is Agreement

You must act with others to present a united front.

Prerequisites: Fame 10, 3 PP.

Benefit: As a full-round action, you can use Intimidate to aid an ally's Bluff or Diplomacy checks (chosen when you gain this award). If you successfully aid another, the bonus added to your ally's check is +3 rather than the normal +2.

Goal: Within 1 week, thwart an investigation into the Brotherhood's connection to a useful politician or business leader without escalating the situation.

Completion Award: Your Fame score increases by 2, and you can use Intimidate to aid an ally on Bluff and Diplomacy checks as a standard action.

LION BLADE SECRET MISSIONS

The Lion Blades are elite spies chosen from the ranks of the prestigious Kitharodian Academy's students to gather information for Taldor and undermine upstart rivals like Andoran and Cheliax.

ESTABLISH AN ASSET

You are directed to an individual in Absalom, Andoran, Cheliax, Galt, Qadira, or Taldor who might prove to be a useful contact for the Lion Blades.

Prerequisites: Fame 5, 1 PP.

Benefit: You gain minor sway with the assigned target (*Ultimate Intrigue* 102).

Goal: Within 1 month, determine the trustworthiness of the target and either secure her aid or blackball her without her realizing she has been investigated by an agent of Taldor.

Completion Award: Your Fame score increases by 1, and you gain moderate sway with the target (*Ultimate Intrigue* 102).

TRAITOR'S STING

You are alerted to a leaked secret and must locate the Lion Blade or ally who leaked it before the trail goes cold.

Prerequisites: Fame 15, 2 PP.

Benefit: You gain a +1 bonus on Stealth checks to hide in crowds and can move through up to 5 feet of difficult terrain caused by crowds each round as if it were normal terrain.

Goal: Within 1 month, eliminate the leak by thwarting a challenging foe.

Completion Award: Your Fame score increases by 2, your bonus on Stealth checks to hide in crowds increases to +2, and you can move through up to 5 feet of difficult terrain caused by crowds as if it were normal terrain.

SCZARNI SECRET MISSIONS

Sczarni crime families, whose members can be found among Varisian wanderers and in big cities like Absalom and Caliphas in Ustalav, are notorious for their skill at blackmail, confidence games, and smuggling.

FAMILY ALIBI

You must cover for a fellow criminal.

Prerequisite: 5 PP.

Benefit: Once per month, you can provide a Sczarni ally with an alibi in the face of criminal charges, making any lies he tells to establish his innocence one step more believable than they otherwise would be. The ally gains a +5 bonus on Bluff checks to establish his innocence of a specific crime.

Goal: Within 1 week, successfully and completely spoil the legal case against a Sczarni member accused of a theft; doing so requires a successful Bluff check (DC = 20 + your level), theft of relevant evidence, a reasonable effort to

frame someone else for their crime, or the elimination of everyone attempting to prosecute your ally.

Completion Award: Your Fame score increases by 2.

OFFICIAL FAVOR

A Sczarni relative asks you to get an official who has been troubling her business to leave off.

Prerequisite: Fame 5.

Benefit: Your relative provides you with information regarding the target's fears and the sorts of bribes that would be persuasive but not overly suspicious, granting you a +2 bonus on Diplomacy checks to bribe the target and Intimidate checks to coerce the target.

Goal: Within 1 month, increase your individual influence (*Ultimate Intrigue* 102) with the target to moderate sway or make the target friendly for at least 1 week, with a skill check DC of at least 20 + your character level.

Completion Award: Your Fame score increases by 1, and the ally secures a valuable smuggling deal; she provides lodging or services (but not crafting or magic item creation) for you worth a total of 100 gp × your Fame score.

WAY OF THE KIRIN SECRET MISSIONS

The Way of the Kirin is a secretive organization dedicated to using business and political power to help the poor and downtrodden without presenting a public target for enemies like the Golden League.

EXPOSE CORRUPTION

You are entrusted with funds to help ferret out corruption.

Prerequisite: 2 PP.

Benefit: You gain free spellcasting services over the next month worth a total of 20 gp × your Fame score, though you must provide any expensive material components or foci.

Goal: Within 1 month, convict an official for corruption, thwarting a foe of a higher level in the process, without revealing your affiliation.

Completion Award: Your Fame score increases by 2, and you gain 1 rank of influence (*Ultimate Intrigue* 109) with any lawful or good organization in Tian Xia.

INDUCTION TEST

You are entrusted with introducing a new member into the Way of the Kirin.

Prerequisites: Fame 15, 2 PP.

Benefit: You are granted the service of a number of Way of the Kirin followers equal to the number of followers you would gain if you had the Leadership feat (minimum one 1st-level follower) for a period of 1 week at the time of your choice.

Goal: Within 1 month, complete a test to evaluate the honor and morality of a potential Way of the Kirin initiate whose level is at least equal to your own without revealing the existence of the group.

Completion Award: Your Fame score increases by 2, and you gain 2 ranks of influence (*Ultimate Intrigue* 109) with one lawful or good organization in Tian Xia.

Secret Agendas

Spies usually have personal goals, ones that might be kept even from trusted allies to avoid the information being used against them in the future.

STORY FEATS

First introduced in *Pathfinder RPG Ultimate Campaign*, story feats give your character a reward for fulfilling a personal goal. For a spy, such a goal requires secrecy to prevent enemy sabotage and often entails the pursuit of hidden information. The full rules for story feats (including definitions for terms like "decisively defeat," "appropriate number," and "challenging foe") can be found on page 66 of *Ultimate Campaign*.

A story feat is gained much like any other feat, but its prerequisites are often nebulous. Each feat's prerequisites can be met multiple ways, subject to GM discretion. As such, you should choose a story feat only after speaking to your GM, so that she can weave the story feat into the campaign's plot or adjust it to fit the context of the campaign. A character needs to meet only one of the listed prerequisites to be eligible to take a feat. Each story feat is also followed by a table that presents possible quests your character might undertake to satisfy the feat's goal. You can choose from the list, or for a surprising challenge, roll on the provided table to select a quest randomly.

ASCENDANT (STORY)

You seek unquestioning admiration and respect to escape from a shameful past.

Prerequisites: You must have the Secret Shame drawback (page 7) or the Bastard-Born background[UCA], and you must also have no publicly known faults or made any indisputable mistakes that could humiliate or cast down a figure of high station.

Benefit: You and your apparent allies gain a +2 bonus on skill checks to gain influence (*Ultimate Intrigue* 102) or request a favor. This bonus no longer applies on checks against a person or organization once you fail a skill check to gain influence over or request a favor from that person or organization. Additionally, the DC of Sense Motive checks to get hunches about you and your apparent allies increases by 2.

Goal: Achieve a position in a high social class (such as the nobility) or an esteemed military position (such as general) without any substantiated rumors impugning your reputation. If your secret is exposed, you can replace this feat with Redemption[UCA] after 1 month without meeting that feat's prerequisite.

Completion Benefit: You no longer lose this feat's bonus for failing a skill check. Your Bluff checks to maintain a good reputation are always at worst unlikely (if not believable), and Bluff checks attempted by others to spoil your reputation are always at best unlikely (if not harder to believe).

d4	Quest
1	Your fellow knights would never let you live it down if they learned you were once a slave and are still technically a fugitive under Chelish law, so you seek a leadership position among the Hellknights, which would make questioning you unthinkable.
2	You stole the identity of a slain Galtan noble to claim the fortune you used to begin your adventuring career, rather than leaving the funds to rot in a foreign Abadaran bank. Now Galtan agents or Abadaran inquisitors threaten to destroy your new life, and you must gain a position of influence strong enough to order them to stop their investigations.
3	You struggle to put your past of piracy or other crimes behind you as you emulate the traditions of the anonymous Ten Magic Warriors in Nantambu and seek a position of power among the Tempest-Sun mages.
4	You found the corpse of a dead linnorm in the Lands of the Linnorm Kings. Since rumors suggest the Linnorm King Opir Eightfingers has already gotten away with pawning off a false victory, you chose to use it to make a claim on the empty throne of Trollheim. You must present your claim and defend yourself from inevitable inquiries into the truth of your conquest.

CONCILIATOR (STORY)

You have witnessed terrible violence and prefer a better way.

Prerequisite: Must have successfully requested that the opposing sides of a violent encounter pause for parley.

Benefit: You can attempt a Diplomacy check to make a request of an enemy even if he is unfriendly or hostile, but only to request a pause in combat (which requires you and your apparent allies to take no attacks or hostile actions for 1 round prior to the request) or to request that he uses only nonlethal attacks (which requires you and your apparent allies to have made no attacks or used only nonlethal attacks against him for the past 24 hours). The DC is equal to 15 + the target's CR + the target's Wisdom modifier; it is modified by any other factors that would impact a Diplomacy check to make a request.

Additionally, your allies within 30 feet who can see or hear you gain a +2 bonus on skill checks to analyze individuals while attempting to gain influence (*Ultimate Intrigue* 102) or assess an audience before a verbal duel (*Ultimate Intrigue* 176). Once an ally benefits from this feat, that ally can't do so again for 1 day.

Goal: Thwart an appropriate number of challenging foes with dialogue, nonviolent favors, and verbal duels.

Completion Benefit: Your allies can benefit from this feat any number of times per day.

d4	Quest
1	You have been sent by Lamasara's Queen Zamere to negotiate an alliance with the Water Lords of Thuvia.
2	You must use speeches to convince the People's Council of Andoran to put an end to the crimes of the Lumber Consortium in Darkmoon Vale.
3	Having witnessed the ceaseless cycle of bloodshed in Galt's vicious overthrows of the government, you are determined to reform or replace the Revolutionary Council without resorting to further violence.
4	You must use negotiation to bring the Cult of the Dawnflower back into the fold and align the members' beliefs and actions to match those of the merciful church of Sarenrae.

INERRANT JUSTICE (STORY)

You will punish the guilty without letting any innocents be harmed as a result.

Prerequisite: Must have witnessed or suffered a grave injustice that went unpunished, or have the An Eye for an Eye[UCA] or the Raiders[UCA] background. If the offender is not a challenging foe, it either advances to become one or allies with one or more creatures who are.

Benefit: Once per day, you can choose to take the maximum possible weapon damage die roll rather than rolling when you hit a foe that is unaware of you or considers you an ally. Bonus dice, including from sneak attack, surprise attack, and Vital Strike, are rolled normally.

Goal: Decisively defeat or slay the offender without killing any innocents in the process. You can complete the goal after killing innocents if you receive an *atonement* spell.

Completion Benefit: You can use this feat's benefit once per combat.

d4	Quest
1	A vigilante such as Blackjack of Korvosa or the Red Raven of Edme took down one of your family members for a crime your relative did not commit, and you must bring that vigilante to justice.
2	You must hunt down the River Kingdoms thugs who defiled sacred elven ruins in Sevenarches.
3	Because your home lacks a strong military force keeping order, as is the case in Riddleport, Kaer Maga, and Numeria, it falls to you to put an end to a serial criminal who preyed upon your friends or family.
4	Katapesh's slave trade through Okeno has ruined countless lives, and you are determined to seek out the kingpin who masterminded this trade from within his luxurious estate and eliminate him.

INFILTRATOR (STORY)

You have sacrificed your true identity in order to achieve your goal.

Prerequisite: Must have adopted an assumed or secret identity associated with an enemy organization.

Benefit: Once per day when you succeed at a saving throw to negate a divination, you learn what the divination would have revealed and can spend an immediate action to cause the divination to return appropriate false information you imagine that would fit with your cover identity.

Goal: Thwart the organization you have infiltrated, defeating or turning to your cause an appropriate number of challenging foes in the process.

Completion Benefit: Whenever a spell or spell-like ability would reveal information about you, you can attempt a Will saving throw. If your saving throw is successful, the spell reveals nothing about you. You can use this feat's benefits to instead give false information, as detailed above.

d4	Quest
1	You must use the rigorous training you received from skilled inquisitors serving Cheliax or the Twilight Talons to join and thwart the Lion Blades.
2	The Conservatory of Grand Sarret in Jalmeray gave you the identity of a distant relative of a rival information broker so you could erase the broker's records and eliminate important witnesses of the Conservatory's psychic spying.
3	Although you were sent as a spy by a ninja clan of Kasai in Minkai, you came to think of your targets as your new kin. When you were caught, you managed to convince your former targets to keep you on as a double agent, and when you were called back to Kasai to report, you went as a spy for your new home.
4	The church of Pharasma assigned you to infiltrate the ranks of the Whispering Way, rumored to be operating out of Ustalav.

MAGICAL ENIGMA (STORY)

A troubling mystery lurks around you, tied to the origin of your magic or your family's legacy, and you seek the truth at all costs.

Prerequisites: Bloodline, eidolon, mystery, phantom, spirit animal, or witch's familiar class feature and you must have an unknown secret about your magic or family history (even if you do not yet know the topic of the secret) or have the One of a Kind[UCA], the Outsider's Lineage[UCA], or the Unknown[UCA] background.

Benefit: Select a class feature from the following list: one bloodline power, eidolon evolutions, one revelation, phantom abilities, spirit animal, or witch's familiar. The feature must be from a class you have at least 1 level in, and you must have the class feature. You can treat either your class level as being 1 higher, or your Intelligence, Wisdom, or Charisma score as 2 higher, for the purpose of calculating the effect of the selected power. This impacts only the calculations of your existing powers that are based on class level or the appropriate ability score. It does not grant you early access to abilities gained at higher levels.

Goal: Learn and verify the chosen magic secret for your family, defeating a challenging foe in the process.

Completion Benefit: Select one Knowledge skill or the Use Magic Device skill. This is now a class skill for you.

d4	Quest
1	You clearly remember briefly having a baby sister, but your family in Illmarsh (in Ustalav) insists she never existed and threatens to cut you off if you do not stop inquiring. Your only clues are your aberrant magical abilities and recurring nightmares of fish-men walking under the surface of the nearby lake.
2	Your eidolon, familiar, or phantom came to you in fulfillment of a bargain it cannot remember and that cannot be revealed to any other mortal lest it come undone, so you quest secretly for its origin.
3	Without seeking it out yourself, you manifested a touch of the divine in godless Rahadoum. You yearn to discover its origin without being imprisoned or executed by the Pure Legion.
4	Your Brevic family's draconic bloodline is secretly said to be linked distantly to the vanished House Rogarvia. You seek to learn Rogarvia's fate and why you were spared without drawing the attention of the many houses intent on usurping Brevoy's throne.

PUPPET MASTER (STORY)

You crave power you can wield without drawing attention to yourself.

Prerequisite: You must have survived an encounter with a challenging foe without suffering significant harm by striking a deal (regardless of whether the deal was with the challenging foe or not), or have the Boss[UCA], the Liege Lord[UCA], or the Well-Connected Friend[UCA] background.

Benefit: If you succeed at a Diplomacy check to make a request of a creature by 5 or more, the DCs of additional requests you attempt increase by 1 per request, rather than 5.

Goal: Either thwart or decisively defeat an appropriate number of challenging foes as a direct result of bargains you have struck or control at least three leaders of settlements of at least 2,000 residents or similarly influential administrators for at least 6 months without being publicly exposed.

Completion Benefit: If you succeed at a Diplomacy check to make a request of a creature, the DCs of additional requests you attempt increase by 1 per request, rather than 5.

d4	Quest
1	You wish to control Isger's leaders in Elidir, who are rumored to be weak and vulnerable to magical manipulation.
2	Your family has suffered humiliation and economic ruin at the hands of the powerful Blakros family in Absalom. You dare not confront them directly, but plan to see to it they believe they are assaulted by enemies on all sides, as you slowly whittle away their influence.
3	You want to manipulate the rulers of the River Kingdoms to gain control of one of the kingdoms, either directly or indirectly.
4	Rumor indicates that Princess Eutropia of Taldor seeks a way to alter the law so she can ascend to the throne when her father Grand Prince Stavian dies. You plan to ensure that she achieves this, and gain her favor and trust in the process.

RIVAL (STORY)

You have a rival, and the two of you try to sabotage, humiliate, or otherwise defeat each other without allowing anyone else to interfere.

Prerequisite: You must have at least one enemy who wishes to outdo you. If you have multiple rivals, the GM may keep the specific rival secret, or have many of your enemies work together against you. If your rival is not already a challenging foe, it either advances to become one or allies itself with others one or more creatures who are.

Benefit: Your striving pushes you to become ever more skillful. When you gain this feat, and every 2 character levels thereafter, either you gain 1 skill point or your Fame score increases by 1 (if your game uses the reputation and Fame system from *Ultimate Campaign*).

Goal: Thwart your rival without anyone else directly interfering. Achieving your rival's goal before her in a manner that humiliates her or completely steals her glory through your direct actions also qualifies.

Completion Benefit: Once per day, you can take 20 on a single skill check as a standard action if the skill check is one that would allow you to take 20.

Special: Thwarting you becomes an all-consuming goal for your rival. Your rival gains a +2 bonus on initiative checks, saving throws, and skill checks against you. Your rival attempts to steal or undermine accomplishments which you strive to achieve.

d4	Quest
1	You and your rival wish to earn entry into the Ruby Phoenix Tournament in Goka, and you must ensure you are victorious.
2	You and an old friend vie for the sole opening at one of the Houses of Perfection in Jalmeray, but only one of you will be accepted.
3	You and a relative with equally distant descent from the Rogarvia family both strive to be the first to unseat King Noleski Surtova and claim rulership of Brevoy.
4	You and a fellow explorer each hope to be the first to reveal a lost dwarven Sky Citadel to the world.

SUPERNATURAL SPY (STORY)

Your familiarity with magic drives you to discover a great supernatural secret. You might work with an eldritch organization, which could be a school of magic such as the Arcanamirium or part of a government with strong ties to magic such as that of Irrisen, or you might attempt to keep your magical inquiries hidden from your employers.

Prerequisites: Alchemist discovery, arcane discovery, arcanist exploit, or magus arcana class feature and you must either have observed a created magical effect you could not understand or have the Master Craftsman^UCA or the Unquenchable Hunger for Knowledge^UCA background.

Benefit: Treat your Intelligence, Wisdom, or Charisma score as 2 higher for the purpose of calculating the effects and save DCs of one of the following class features: alchemist discoveries, arcane discoveries, arcanist exploits, or magus arcana. You select both the ability score and class feature to be affected when you select this feat, and the choice cannot be changed. This increases the potency of the abilities but does not grant access to additional abilities.

Goal: Learn a great supernatural secret, connected in some manner to an aspect of the class feature you selected with this story feat. You must evade or thwart a challenging foe in the process.

Completion Benefit: When calculating the effect of the class feature selected with this feat, you treat your class level for the relevant class as 2 higher. This does not impact when you gain access to additional abilities tied to that class feature, only the effectiveness of abilities from the feature you already have.

d4	Quest
1	Members of the Bureau of Criers show up near occult phenomena with suspicious frequency; you seek to learn what they have learned on

a major topic such as extraplanetary studies, necrotic enrichment, or supernatural meteorology.

2	Aboleths are rumored to use gillmen and other servants (both knowing and unwitting) to monitor or manipulate events in Absalom, and you intend to discover more about the aboleth ability to transform other creatures.
3	You seek to discover the terms of the infernal pact used by Queen Abrogail I to secure House Thrune's rule over Cheliax to learn more about infernal magic.
4	An Osirian priest of Nethys charges you with hunting down a powerful divination spell lost long ago and rumored to have been found and sold by merchants from Andoran to an unknown Nexian buyer.

WILY WARRIOR (STORY)

Those who observe your imposing demeanor assume muscle is your sole advantage, but you prove them wrong every time.

Prerequisite: Bluff 1 rank, Sense Motive 1 rank, base attack bonus +1, or you must have the Military Strategist background (page 5).

Benefit: Once per day, you can use your ranks in Sense Motive in place of your total Will saving throw modifier when attempting a Will save. You must decide to use this ability prior to attempting the saving throw.

Goal: Thwart an appropriate number of challenging foes after getting a negative hunch about them when they attempted to deceive you or after ambushing them.

Completion Benefit: The DC of Bluff and Intimidate checks attempted against you increase by 5.

d4	Quest
1	You were born and raised in Trunau in the Hold of Belkzen, a town surrounded and often besieged by orcs (and occasionally giants), and will defend it against all attackers.
2	Your awareness was honed to a knife's edge by training in Jalmeray's martial monasteries, and you wish to outdo every rival.
3	You serve under (or with) the Risen Guard of Osirion to steadfastly watch for spies and assassins seeking to undermine Ruby Prince Khemet III.
4	Foolish Molthuni commanders have proven themselves temporary but relentless problems for Nirmathas. You intend to give them a humiliating defeat that will finally put them in their place.

Information Dealing

Information is the stock and trade of spies. Many gather secrets with their own skills and contacts and use them only to advance the causes of their patrons. But some spies see information as a commodity, buying and selling it as a merchant would trade silk or iron. Information dealing provides spies an avenue to turn stolen secrets into liquid assets. Similarly, it allows a spy to delegate her work and purchase available information when she can't spare the time to seek it out herself.

To the right buyer, a secret can be just as dangerous and valuable as a rare magic item. As a result, certain pieces of information can be bought much like magic items and sold for half the market price. However, even more so than magic items, a secret's availability is, by definition, limited.

BUYING SECRETS

These rules are only for buying information unknown to even the most learned of the general public, but known to someone willing to part with the knowledge for money or services. Generally, if it's possible to recall information with the Knowledge skill or learn it with certainty by gathering information with the Diplomacy skill (regardless of the check's DC), that information can be easily acquired by hiring a sage rather than going to an information broker. Similarly, it is impossible to spend money to find out details about the death of the god Aroden or what's at the center of the Eye of Abendego, because either no one knows the answers or those who do will never part with such secrets. The GM is the final arbiter of whether a piece of information is for sale and how much it costs.

Price of Power: The price of a secret is loosely linked to the power of those concerned with keeping it secret or intent on discovering it. A secret's market price is generally equal to the CR of the most powerful creature wishing to keep it a secret × that same CR × 100 gp. The use of the most powerful keeper of a secret represents the risk involved in dealing with such secrets. Even if only a few lesser Hellknights are tasked with keeping a minor Chelish state secret from the public, if Abrogail Thrune has taken a person interest in punishing anyone who sells the secret, any information broker who learns it will demand top dollar.

The base price of information is also modified according to the secret's prominence. Determining this price is more art than science, much like for a magic item, so the GM decides its final market price (and whether it can be effectively purchased at all). Outside of the area where a secret could reasonably be learned or where it could have a major impact on local matters, a secret generally costs twice as much as usual. The DC of an Appraise check to determine the value of a secret is approximately 15 + CR of the secret's greatest keeper. The prominence of the person, place, or thing that the secret is about can alter this DC as indicated on the table below.

Prominence: There's a reason spies often say two people can keep a secret if one of them is dead. The prominence of information to be bought or sold, based on how many people can reasonably be considered to know it, affects the skill check DCs and the secret's price. The number of creatures that know a piece of information is merely a guideline for determining a secret's prominence. A GM might decide that even if 200 monks all know the true identity of a rebel leader, their vows of silence and oaths to protect that leader mean the secret is still isolated.

Secret Prominence	Number of Creatures That Know It	Appraise DC Modifier	Price Modifier
Isolated	Fewer than 5	+5	+50%
Uncommon	6–20	+2	+25%
Known	21–200	+0	+0%
Open secret	201+	−5	−25%

Finding a Seller: Finding an information broker selling a specific secret is a tricky process. A character can determine if the information is likely to be for sale by someone in a given settlement with a successful Knowledge check appropriate to the topic of the secret, or a successful Diplomacy check to gather information. The DC of such a check is equal to the DC of an Appraise check to determine that secret's value. Until characters discover that such a check can be bought, the GM should roll this check in secret. If the check is successful, but the GM has already determined that no one has this piece of information for sale, the character knows looking for a broker is pointless.

If the information is for sale, the GM can determine the chance it's available in a specific settlement. If the value of the secret is equal to or less than the settlement's base value

Sample Secrets

Secret	Appraise DC	Suggested Market Price
Chelish histories dating from before the Chelish Civil War	25	67,500 gp
Details of the *sun orchid elixir*'s next escort	24	16,100 gp
The crimes and location of an escaped traitor or criminal	15 + escapee's CR	escapee's HD squared × 50 gp + prominence modifier
The identity of an undercover spy	15 + spy's CR	spy's HD squared × 50 gp + prominence modifier
Proof of a survivable political scandal	15 + politician's CR	(politician's HD + prominence modifier) squared × 50 gp
Proof of a ruinous political scandal	15 + politician or patron's CR	(politician's HD + prominence modifier) squared × 100 gp
Prototype firearm schematics	25	6,400 gp

(*Pathfinder RPG GameMastery Guide* 205), there's a 50% chance the secret is available for sale there. If the secret's value is up to double a settlement's base value, there's a 45% chance it's available for sale. For every additional doubling required to bring the base value up to the cost of the secret, the chance of it being available is reduced by an additional 5%.

Once a character knows a given piece of information is likely available for sale, he must find and contact the selling information broker. Finding an information broker or other seller with a specific secret requires a successful Diplomacy check to gather information with a DC equal to the DC of the Appraise check to determine its value. Because most information brokers rely on secrecy of the topics being discussed for their livelihoods and safety, it's also necessary to succeed at a DC 15 Bluff or Knowledge (local) check to find the seller without spooking her or raising the interest of groups opposed to the sale of the information. On a failed check, the broker may demand proof the PCs aren't being followed before agreeing to a meeting, or the characters may be attacked by other groups interested in the same secret.

Selling Secrets: Just as they can be bought, secrets can be sold. Only information that is not known to even the most learned of the general public can be sold, and the GM is the final arbiter of whether anyone is interested in buying a secret and how much they are willing to pay for it. In general, players should assume a piece of information gleaned through skill checks is never a secret worth selling (if the player can learn it without risk and effort, so can other creatures). However, a GM can choose to grant PCs valuable secrets as rewards for adventures. This can be a good way to add value to a trove without giving away yet more coins, *potions of cure light wounds*, and masterwork short swords. Like magic items, a secret can generally be sold for half its value, and the amount a settlement can pay for an item is limited by the settlement's purchase limit (*GameMastery Guide* 205). A GM may decide to allow players to seek a buyer willing to pay full price for a secret, which is generally about as difficult as finding someone willing and able to sell a secret.

Devalued Secrets: Secrets retain their value only as long as not everyone knows them. If a seller doesn't convincingly assure a buyer he won't sell the same secret to others, the price a buyer is willing to pay goes down (to as little as 10% of the secret's value). In some cases, this is a simple matter, as the secret is tied to some object that acts as proof of its veracity and the object cannot be easily duplicated. For example, if a major noble in Taldor has lost a crucial piece of family jewelry, possession of that jewelry is proof enough of the claim that it's missing. When selling that secret, selling the jewelry itself along with an explanation of how the noble came to lose it is likely ample proof the secret won't be resold. Even if someone tried to sell it again, they lack the damning evidence to prove the claim.

In many other cases, a secret is easy to copy, and some level of trust must be established between buyer and seller. If the seller has a long-term relationship with an information broker, verbal assurances are likely enough to allow a sale, though if such trust is ever lost, it is very difficult to restore. This is tends to be an option only with brokers who have attitudes of friendly or helpful toward a seller of secrets. For transactions between parties with less well-established relationships, a Diplomacy check with the same DC that would be required to improve the buyer's attitude by one step is often enough to establish the seller's good intentions. If the seller does plan to double-cross the buyer, a successful Bluff check opposed by the buyer's Sense Motive is required.

If a check to establish trust fails by 5 or less, the buyer can still purchase the secret at a reduced price if some kind of guarantee can be established (which might be as simple as the lingering threat of hunting down the seller if the secret turns up anywhere else). A check that fails by 5 or more indicates the buyer is simply unwilling to purchase the secret at all.

Similarly, if a secret is rendered useless or irrelevant (such as if the person it grants power over dies or disappears), it becomes worthless. Some secrets may be of value only within a specific time frame—the battle plan of an enemy army is quite valuable, but only until the battle is over.

Sample Secrets: Listed in the table above are typical market prices for secrets that might be discovered across Golarion. These prices are only examples; the GM determines if a piece of information can be bought or sold and at what price.

Spies of Golarion

Countless groups throughout the Inner Sea region and beyond vie for valuable secrets and to thwart the probing eyes of competitors. These organizations often see all other information-gathering networks as rivals, even if they're not true political enemies, but are also willing to forge short-term alliances should a common foe gain an upper hand. The intense secrecy and high-stakes nature of the work performed by these groups' agents often lead to the development of specialized training, talents, and tools used to achieve their goals in the most efficient and effective manner possible.

BLACKJACKETS

Druma's mercenary Blackjackets are easily the best-funded private military organization within the Inner Sea region.

They use their considerable magical and martial resources to protect the interests of the Kalistocrats who keep them on retainer. Drumish caravans across the region hire Blackjackets to catch devious thieves and spies who would steal vital information or carry out ruinous heists. The Blackjackets' enemies include most spy and criminal organizations, which are generally highly cautious around the Kalistocrats' agents, especially since stories indicate even incredibly powerful magic is of little to no use in confounding their well-equipped soldiers. The Blackjackets take special care to watch for spies when guarding Kalistocrats hired as mediators or diplomats, since such clients are often called into disputes of extremely sensitive and far-reaching matters.

The following item is available to anyone who has served with the Blackjackets.

UNTOUCHABLE JACKET		PRICE 18,000 GP
SLOT body	**CL** 9th	**WEIGHT** 1 lb.
AURA moderate abjuration		

This black jacket is marked with the insignia of the Blackjackets. Once per day, the wearer can speak a command word to gain spell resistance 20 for 3 rounds. This spell resistance ends if the wearer successfully resists a spell as a result of it failing to penetrate his spell resistance. The first time each day that a spell has no effect on the wearer because of spell resistance or a successful saving throw, the jacket becomes charged with abjuration magic and its insignia glows faintly. The wearer can touch the glowing insignia as a standard action to cast *dispel magic* from the jacket, expending the charge. The charge fades with no effect if unused for 1 hour.

CONSTRUCTION REQUIREMENTS	**COST** 9,000 GP

Craft Wondrous Item, *dispel magic*, *spell resistance*

BROTHERHOOD OF SILENCE

The largest thieves' guild in the Inner Sea region, the Brotherhood of Silence is based in Oppara and has chapter houses in many cities across the land. Beholden to no one, the group steals information as well as more tangible wares. Its members favor quick pay-offs and blackmailing schemes that are alarmingly effective. A typical extortion involves masked Brotherhood thugs threatening to reveal embarrassing secrets burgled from lovers' bedrooms or snatched from messengers; when the price is paid, the evidence is safely returned. The Brotherhood's renowned silence extends to blackmail that has been paid in full, and is enforced violently upon upstart members who attempt to get extra "off the books" pay or sell valuable evidence to other buyers, such as the church of Calistria or the Guild of Wonders in Absalom.

The Brotherhood is reputed to have agents in every city, major organization, and noble house in the Inner Sea region. In truth, most Brotherhood spies simply use magic to take on any appearance needed to complete difficult missions. Any rogue can select the following talent. Investigators and slayers can also select this talent if they have the Brute, Failed Apprentice, Militia Veteran, Rapscallion, River Rat, Vagabond Child, or Well-Informed trait from *Pathfinder RPG Advanced Player's Guide*, or Narrows Survivor or Wealthy Dabbler trait from *Pathfinder Player Companion: Taldor, Echoes of Glory*.

One of Those Faces (Sp): Each day, you can use *disguise self* as a spell-like ability for up to 10 minutes per character level. This duration need not be continuous, but it must be used in 10-minute increments. Additionally, once you have used this ability, whenever you use it for the next 24 hours you must take the same alternate appearance.

THE CONSERVATORY

The Conservatory of Grand Sarret trains the greatest spies of Jalmeray in psychic disciplines while preparing them to be the most sought-after and skilled companions of the entire Inner Sea region. Members become hosts, cooks, diplomats, musicians, artists, and trusted confidants to aristocrats, nobles, and even queens and kings. The Conservatory's existence is a closely guarded secret, so its members must constantly take care not to reveal their connection to the supposedly abandoned island of Grand Sarret.

Some skilled mesmerists within the Conservatory have even learned to conceal the presence of others when engaged in spycraft. The following feat is available to anyone who meets its prerequisites.

OBLIVIATING STARE (STARE)

Your stare can cause a target to lose track of someone.

Prerequisites: Allure bold stare improvement (*Pathfinder RPG Occult Adventures* 42), hypnotic stare class feature (*Occult Adventures* 39), Mesmerist level 5th.

Benefit: You can cause a target of your hypnotic stare to lose track of creatures other than yourself. If the target of your hypnotic stare is in an environment that would allow the target to take 10 on skill checks (if not in immediate danger or distracted), creatures can attempt Stealth checks opposed by the target's Perception check even if they lack cover or concealment. If the target of your hypnotic stare fails an opposed Perception check by 5 or more, it forgets the creature attempting the Stealth check was ever present, and acts as if it had failed a Will saving throw against a *hidden presence*[UI] spell cast by the creature using Stealth. If your hypnotic stare ends, the target takes damage, a creature using Stealth takes an action that would end a *hidden presence* spell, or the target's circumstances change so it would be unable to take 10 on a skill check, all effects of Obliviating Stare end and the target is immune to your Obliviating Stare for 24 hours.

GOLDEN LEAGUE

The Golden League is a criminal organization with agents and houses across the Dragon Empires. Its main business interests involve gambling and thievery, commonly pinned on innocent patsies to throw off investigators. Although the Golden League readily victimizes the poor, it insulates itself from personal or governmental reprisal by helping the downtrodden residing near its bases of operation—so long as they demonstrate loyalty to the League. At the same time, its members swiftly punish anyone who helps the authorities oppose them. Agents proclaim their rank with proudly displayed tattoos. The Golden League's chief enemies are the Way of the Kirin and strong, good-aligned Tian governments.

Golden League agents can select the following feat.

GOLDEN LEAGUE TATTOOS

You have quite the impressive collection of tattoos that commemorate your connection to and achievements within the Golden League.

Prerequisite: Regional trait associated with one of the Dragon Empires nations (*Pathfinder Player Companion: Dragon Empires Primer*).

Benefit: You have an impressive collection of tattoos, which are visible unless you wear concealing clothing or succeed at a DC 10 Disguise check. You can take 10 on Intimidate checks against creatures able to see your tattoos, even when stress or distractions would normally prevent you from doing so. You add Knowledge (local) to the skills associated with the presence tactic for verbal duels (*Pathfinder RPG Ultimate Intrigue*), and the first time you win an exchange with that tactic you do not take a penalty on associated skill checks if you repeat the tactic in the same duel.

GUARDIANS OF IMMORTALITY

The Guardians of Immortality combine the resources of the five city-states of Thuvia to protect their shared asset: the *sun orchid elixir*. These spies train in varied techniques to root out and foil plots against their most precious resource. Many guardians of immortality adopt the guardian of immortality investigator archetype (*Pathfinder Campaign Setting: Inner Sea Intrigue* 41).

Guardians of immortality have developed the following alchemist[APG] discovery, though it has since been carefully studied by other alchemists and can be selected by any alchemist who meets its prerequisite.

Glimmering Infusion (Sp): The alchemist can expend any prepared extract to produce a cube of glowing motes that act as per *glitterdust*. The area must be adjacent to the alchemist and covers one 5-foot square per level of extract sacrificed, and the effect's save DC is calculated using the level of the sacrificed extract. The alchemist must have the infusion discovery to choose this discovery.

HERALDS OF SUMMER'S RETURN

The Heralds of Summer's Return watch the White Witches who rule Irrisen with an iron grasp, looking for weaknesses, valuable magical secrets, and potential turncoats. These rebels are scattered and ill-organized, and have not yet discovered how to break the spell of eternal winter over their land. They

also seek secret ways to gain support from the Lands of the Linnorm Kings without detection by Irrisen's magical border wardens. The group's members are predominantly druids, rogues, and other classes who can hide in the wilderness or back streets without drawing attention.

Heralds of Summer's Return can select the following trait.

Winter Witchcraft Survivor (Magic): You narrowly escaped death when a Winter Witch punished you for supporting the Heralds. You gain cold resistance 5 against the first cold damage you take each day, and gain a +2 bonus on saving throws against the fear effects of creatures with the cold subtype.

MAGAAMBYA

The Magaambya, the oldest school of magical learning in the Inner Sea region, has allowed the city of Nantambu to establish an oasis of relative safety and peace in the midst of the chaotic Mwangi Expanse through remarkable diplomacy, magical prowess, and counterintelligence. Arcanists, druids, explorers, and scholars of many sorts watch for spies from across the Mwangi Expanse and beyond. Such enemy spies are often associated with the Aspis Consortium, demon cultists, and warlike Mwangi settlements, including Mzali. Magaambya agents use divinations and shapeshifting disguises, allowing unhelpful information to escape and violently expelling spies who threaten to reveal the city's strategic weak points or steal vital magical knowledge.

The following spell is most common among spellcasters educated at the Magaambya.

WATCHFUL ANIMAL

School divination (scrying); **Level** druid 4, ranger 4, shaman 4, sorcerer/wizard 4, witch 4
Casting Time 10 minutes
Components V, S, M/DF (a desiccated fly)
Range medium (100 ft. plus 10 ft./level)
Effect magical sensor
Duration 10 minutes/level
Saving Throw none; **Spell Resistance** no

You place a scrying sensor on your animal companion or familiar. This allows the animal companion or familiar to function as if it were an insect summoned by the *greater insect spy*[UI] spell. The animal companion or familiar does not change shape, nor does it lose the ability to make its own decisions, but it receives orders and gives answers as per insects summoned by that spell, and you can sense its direction and distance and receive sensory input from it as with that spell.

MENDEVIAN CRUSADE

The Mendevian Crusade is targeted by spies representative of a variety of groups, and trains inquisitors to catch these false crusaders in their ranks. Demons and their cultists frequently attempt to infiltrate the crusade to undermine the war effort and tear the Worldwound wider. Witches and druids from the Estrovian Forest, Technic League agents from Numeria, and opportunists who do not take the demonic threat seriously spy on the crusade for any opportunity to limit the movement's power, steal supplies, or fleece crusaders.

The need to weed out potential false followers has led to the development of specific forms of divine magic. The following spell is most common among spellcasters serving the Mendevian Crusade.

TRIAL BY FIRE

School evocation [fire]; **Level** antipaladin 3, cleric 3, inquisitor 3, paladin 3
Casting Time 1 standard action
Components V, S, DF
Range touch
Target creature touched
Duration instantaneous
Saving Throw None; **Spell Resistance** yes

You test a creature's purity of convictions by exposing it to a sheet of divine fire. Unless the target's alignment is within one step of your deity's, the spell deals 1d6 points of damage per 2 caster levels (maximum 5d6 points of damage). Half the damage is fire damage, but the other half results directly from divine power and is therefore not subject to being reduced by resistance to fire-based attacks. Additionally, if the target has an element of its alignment that is in direct opposition to your (chaos opposes law and evil opposes good), you can also attempt an Intimidate check to demoralize the target as a free action.

DRAGONSHADOW

A clan of deadly ninja headquartered in Minkai, the Dragonshadow has placed agents throughout trade networks to many parts of Golarion, including Absalom, Goka, Jalmeray, and Katapesh. Dragonshadow ninja use prophecies from their hidden imperial dragon ancestor to keep the clan strong and gain new assets like lost artifacts, and use sorcery to augment their secret missions. Infighting is common among this clan, and leadership disputes could be settled in honorable duels or through stealthy assassinations. For more information on the Dragonshadow clan, see *Pathfinder Adventure Path #52: Forest of Spirits*.

Members of the Dragonshadow developed the following ninja trick[UC], which can be selected by any ninja.

Breath of the Ancestor (Su): The ninja chooses one imperial dragon type (forest, sea, sky, sovereign, or underworld; *Pathfinder RPG Bestiary 3* 92–103) when she gains this trick, and the choice can't be changed. She can use supplies similar to those used for ninja smoke bombs to produce an alchemical breath weapon that deals the same kind of damage as the selected dragon (piercing damage for forest dragons, fire for sea dragons, and so on). The breath weapon deals the same amount of damage as the ninja's sneak attack, with a Reflex save allowed for half damage. The breath weapon is a 15-foot cone (or a 30-foot line if the underworld dragon is selected). The save DC is equal to 10 + 1/2 the ninja's class level + the ninja's Intelligence modifier. Using this ability is a standard action that expends up 2 ki points, and once used it cannot be used again for 1d4 rounds.

PURE LEGION

The nation of Rahadoum steadfastly bans the worship and service of any deity to protect its people from religious war and other crimes committed on behalf of the gods. Rahadoum's Pure Legion watches vigilantly for any divine servants violating the Laws of Man. Many religious groups send spies and seditionists to undermine this atheistic nation and, in turn, Pure Legion agents guard the borders and investigate potential hidden cults. In addition, the Pure Legion quietly sends members to devoted nations to study recent changes in religious practices and identify those conspiring to violate Rahadoum's laws—although they take care not to create international incidents when operating beyond their obvious authority. The Pure Legion also studies methods of combating divine power, leading some who have studied with the Pure Legion to take the following feat.

PURE LEGION ASSAULT (COMBAT)

The Pure Legion trained you to apply your knowledge of religions to predicting and defeating divine servitors.

Prerequisites: Bluff 1 rank, Knowledge (religion) 1 rank, Pure Legion Recruit trait (*Pathfinder Player Companion: People of the Sands* 21).

Benefit: You gain a +2 bonus on saving throws against divine spells and effects and abilities from outsiders. If you must attempt a saving throw against a divine spell, you gain a +1 bonus on attack rolls against the creature that cast the spell.

STARWATCH

Based out of Starwatch Keep to the east of Absalom, the Starwatch is charged with executing the will of Absalom's Grand Council, a task that includes alerting the Council to spies in the city. At the orders of feuding councilors, individual members of the Starwatch are often assigned tasks meant to be secret even from the rest of the Starwatch. Less scrupulous members see these as opportunities to earn prestige from those councilors and perhaps a promotion, even if the city is made less safe as a result. The Starwatch must be wary of crossing that line, however, since Absalom's First Guard retains the right to exile the Starwatch if the safety of the city is at stake.

Spies in Absalom often work with the Arcanamirium or one of the local cognates to receive training in recognizing and avoiding magic sensors. The following talent can be taken by any rogue, investigator, or slayer.

Scrying Familiarity (Ex): You are well acquainted with scrying sensors. You can roll twice and take the better result on saving throws against divination (scrying) spells and effects, on Perception checks to notice scrying sensors, and on caster level checks to overcome spell resistance when you use a scrying spell or effect. If you notice a magical sensor, you can attempt a Stealth check opposed by the caster's caster level check to avoid being detected by the sensor.

WINTER COUNCIL

The Winter Council is dismissed as a conspiracy theory by most of Kyonin, but it does exist. The organization endeavors to stop spies and dissidents from endangering the elven land. Its stated role is to protect Kyonin from threats to its culture and stability. Although it is connected to the Lantern Bearers, its interests extend beyond the threat of the drow to foreign spies, malign supernatural influences, and domestic rabble-rousers. Its agents discreetly keep the secrets of the elves away from non-elves, even if that sometimes requires eliminating a few rebellious elves in the process.

The following wizard arcane discovery[UM] is available to elven wizards and wizard servants of the Winter Council in place of a feat.

Observant Illusion (Su): You can project your senses into any ongoing figment or shadow illusion you create with a spell of at least 3rd level. You can see through its eyes and hear through its ears as if you were standing where it is, and during your turn you can switch from using its senses to using your own, or back again, as a swift or move action. While you are using its senses, your body is considered blinded and deafened. You must be at least a 9th-level wizard to choose this discovery.

Vigilantes of Golarion

Whether skulking through dim alleyways or prowling about lavish parties, vigilantes are found almost exclusively in centers of humanoid culture and society, for their dualistic natures and talents are at their pinnacle within such environs. As diverse in ability as they are secretive, most vigilantes act alone and pursue personal agendas, be they well-intended or psychotic. As a result, vigilantes can be found across Golarion, lurking in plain sight as they plot and scheme to further their own ends, or those of their masters.

Absalom: Befitting its title as the City in the Center of the World, Absalom boasts the largest social and political scene in the Inner Sea region. With so many interests and agendas in conflict, the metropolis spawns countless vigilantes, dedicated to all manner of causes and creeds and often engaged in a constant shadowy war against one another. Many of the city's established vigilantes command their own gangs or attract circles of neophyte masked personas to spread their reach across the massive city and the nations it influences.

Arcadia: Across the Arcadian Ocean from the Inner Sea region, the continent of Arcadia features its own empires and city-states teeming with political strife and hidden plans. The city of Segada (*Pathfinder Campaign Setting: Distant Shores* 44) sees a number of agendas and traditions in conflict that spawn their own vigilantes.

Avistan: The Avistani peoples are known to be quite individualistic, and many resent any authority that interferes with their lives. This inclination produces more vigilantes per capita than anywhere else on Golarion. This isn't necessarily a good thing, as for every masked freedom fighter rising up against Chelish tyranny or defending the peasantry from the White Witches of Irrisen, there is also a royalist undermining democratic efforts on Galt's blood-soaked streets or a priest of Razmir spreading his false faith across the Lake Encarthan region.

Garund: Garund has fewer modern vigilantes who hail from its population centers or serve political agendas, but features a long history of masked champions dating back to Old-Mage Jatembe and the Ten Magic Warriors. Most of the continent's vigilantes emulate this tradition of wandering masked champions by becoming traveling adventurers, dividing their social and vigilante identities to the point where these aspects become distinct personalities—two souls, sometimes at odds, sharing the same body.

Qadira: Qadira's vigilantes often take up a mask to avoid the restrictions of their social or economic positions to become folk heroes—living as travelers, traders, and pilgrims by day, but taking on roles as incredible thieves, legendary assassins, or champions of the defenseless who come and go with the night. Equally common are those who secretly support a more organized group, such as secretive agents of the Cult of the Dawnflower—Sarenrae's militant offshoot church—who serve as humble priests by day and push their cult's aggressive agendas by night.

Tian Xia: When the Lung Wa empire collapsed, much of Tian Xia was left without justice or protection on a local level, spawning countless local heroes and vigilantes, though this legacy is beginning to fade as the political climate has stabilized over the past century. Only Goka—a great trade city hosting countless gangs, trading companies, and overlapping jurisdictions—and the tengu nation of Kwanlai—where commoners struggle to find justice and battle official corruption—still have strong traditions of seeking redress from behind the anonymity of a mask.

VIGILANTE ARCHETYPES

The following vigilante archetypes represent specialized forms of vigilantism found throughout the Inner Sea region. Although each archetype is often associated with a specific organization or region in the Inner Sea, all of these archetypes have since be adapted by others and spread across Golarion and beyond.

AGATHIEL (VIGILANTE ARCHETYPE)

The legends of Golarion teem with intelligent beasts who emerge from the wild to right wrongs perpetrated by a nation, aid a virtuous family, or extract long-overdue vengeance. Many of these trace back to the agathiel tradition, first stolen from agathion celestials by the elves of Kyonin and again later by Old-Mage Jatembe. Agathiels surrender a portion of their immortal souls to Nirvana in exchange for a measure of animalistic might to aid them in their righteous crusades. This exchange is permanent, and each agathiel commits the rest of his mortal life to service of others and the constant thrum of wild instincts.

Though agathiels can be found in small numbers all over Golarion, the rituals to transform a mortal into an agathiel are common only in Kyonin and the Mwangi city-states, and among the wandering scholars of the Mwangi Expanse. The elves in particular relied upon these abilities to scout Golarion before reclaiming their abandoned territories after the Age of Darkness, leading to reports of extraordinary fey animals stalking elven ruins in the century before their return.

Immortal Commitment (Su): Becoming an agathiel commits a portion of the vigilante's soul to Nirvana, and in turn invests him with a portion of the plane's power. An agathiel's social and vigilante identity alignments must both be within one step of neutral good. If either of the agathiel's alignments moves outside this range (because of his own actions or magical manipulation), he gains 1 permanent negative level and loses the ability to assume his vigilante identity until both of his alignments are within one step of neutral good. This negative level cannot be overcome in any way (including by *restoration* spells) until the agathiel's alignment reverts.

Bestial Identity (Su): At 1st level, an agathiel's vigilante identity must invoke the appearance and behavior of a single Small or Medium creature of the animal type. The vigilante can attempt to appear to be a normal member of this animal type, but doing so imposes a –10 penalty on his Disguise check. The bonus provided by seamless guise still applies to the vigilante's attempts to appear to be an ordinary animal. Once the vigilante's animal form is selected, it cannot be changed.

Beginning at 4th level, when an agathiel assumes his vigilante identity, he physically transforms into an animal, though he always retains unusual traits that set him apart from ordinary animals, as if using *beast shape I*, except the vigilante gains no ability adjustments and can select only a single animal ability from those listed in the spell's description. His social identity remains his true form,

and unlike with *beast shape I*, an agathiel can remain in his animal form indefinitely. The agathiel's vigilante identity is considered a polymorph effect, and while in his vigilante identity, the agathiel is immune to other polymorph effects. Unlike with normal polymorph effects, the agathiel's equipment does not meld into his form, and instead changes shape to fit his animal form and provides the same function, though any equipment requiring hands cannot be used until he returns to his social identity.

At 8th level, when assuming his vigilante identity, the vigilante can select two abilities provided by *beast shape I*, or select a single ability provided by *beast shape II*. At 12th level, he can instead select two abilities provided by *beast shape II*, or a single ability provided by *beast shape III*. At 16th level, he can instead select three abilities provided by *beast shape III*, or a single ability provided by *beast shape IV*.

This ability alters dual identity and replaces the vigilante talents gained at 4th, 8th, 12th, and 16th levels.

Agathion Blessing (Su): Beginning at 2nd level, an agathiel gains Aspect of the Beast[APG] as a bonus feat while in his vigilante identity. If he selects the claws of the beast option, he can select a bite attack (1d8), a gore attack (1d8), or 2 slam attacks (1d4 each), as appropriate to his animal identity.

This ability replaces the vigilante talent gained at 2nd level.

BELLFLOWER HARVESTER (VIGILANTE ARCHETYPE)

Bellflower harvesters are the front-line operatives of the secretive Bellflower Network, whose members infiltrate Chelish estates in the guise of servants and slaves, and tolerate a harsh life as they uncover secrets, gauge security, and send slaves on the first steps towards freedom. While Bellflower tillers (*Pathfinder Campaign Setting: Paths of Prestige* 10) wander the countryside, escorting the crop of escapees to freedom, the harvester remains in seeming bondage to direct others to the road to freedom, undermine efforts to recapture slaves, and end the threat of especially vile masters.

Bellflower harvesters consist almost exclusively of halflings, though the role could be taken by anyone with the patience or humility to withstand months or years of cruel abuse without risking being caught raising a hand in his own defense.

Rebellious Identity (Ex): A Bellflower harvester's vigilante identity must be within one step of chaotic good, and his social identity must appear to be a slave, servant, or other menial laborer.

This alters dual identity.

Bellflower Crop (Ex): A Bellflower harvester can designate a number of allies equal to 3 + his Charisma modifier as part of his Bellflower crop. Members of a Bellflower crop must remain within 30 feet of the Bellflower harvester in order to gain the benefits granted by a Bellflower harvester's other class abilities as detailed below; if they leave this range, the Bellflower harvester must designate these allies again for them to be included in his crop.

When the Bellflower harvester uses the aid another action to grant a member of his Bellflower crop a bonus on an attack roll against an opponent, on a skill check, or to AC against an opponent's next attack, the bonus increases to +3. This doesn't stack with the benefits of other feats or class features that improve the bonus he grants to an ally with aid another. At 5th level and every 6 vigilante levels thereafter, the bonus that the Bellflower harvester provides when using aid another to assist a member of his Bellflower crop increases by 1, to a maximum of +6 at 17th level.

This ability replaces vigilante specialization.

Obsequious (Ex): A Bellflower harvester works hard to cultivate a social identity that plays off others' racist assumptions to deflect blame and excuse suspicious behavior, making him seem harmless or even a model servant. He can use the Bluff skill to deflect suspicion about his vigilante identity and activities (including use of vigilante talents when in his social identity) rather than Disguise, and gains a +2 bonus on Bluff checks to do so. This bonus increases by 1 for every 4 vigilante levels he has beyond 1st, to a maximum of +6 at 17th level.

This ability replaces the social talent gained at 1st level.

Tend the Garden (Ex): Beginning at 2nd level, a Bellflower harvester gains the ability to coordinate his Bellflower crop to improve their performance in battle. He gains Stealth Synergy[UC] as a bonus feat. As a standard action, a Bellflower harvester can grant any one teamwork feat he has to all members of his Bellflower crop who can see and hear him. Members of his Bellflower crop retain this feat for 1 round, plus 1 round for every 5 vigilante levels the Bellflower harvester has beyond 2nd, to a maximum of 4 rounds at 17th level. A Bellflower harvester can share only one teamwork feat at a time in this manner.

This ability replaces the vigilante talent gained at 6th level.

Social Talents: The following social talents complement the Bellflower harvester: case the joint[UI], feign innocence[UI], gossip collector[UI], loyal aid[UI], and subjective truth[UI].

Vigilante Talents: The following vigilante talents complement the Bellflower harvester: blind spot[UI], environment weapon[UI], shadow's sight[UI], and team player (see page 27).

Teisatsu (Vigilante Archetype)

Teisatsu are specialized vigilantes who focus on infiltrating social scenes and high-society gatherings on behalf of the feuding lords of Minkai. Trained as assassins and spies, they cultivate a suite of personalities and study secret arts that hone their bodies into deadly weapons.

Weapon and Armor Proficiency: Teisatsu are proficient with all simple weapons, plus the kama, katana, kusarigama, nunchaku, sai, short sword, shortbow, shuriken, siangham, and wakizashi. They are proficient with light and medium armor, but not with shields.

This replaces the vigilante's normal weapon and armor proficiencies.

Infiltrator (Ex): A teisatsu is required to choose stalker as his specialization.

This alters vigilante specialization.

Ki Pool (Su): At 2nd level, a teisatsu gains a ki pool, identical to the ninja class feature (*Pathfinder RPG Ultimate Combat* 14), using his vigilante level as his effective ninja level.

This ability replaces the vigilante talent gained at 2nd level.

Teisatsu Talents: A teisatsu selects vigilante talents as normal. He can't select the rogue talent vigilante talent. He can, however, select either of the talents below, which are unique to the teisatsu.

This ability alters vigilante talents.

Ki Power (Su): The teisatsu gains a single ki power of his choice from the list available to the unchained monk class (*Pathfinder RPG Pathfinder Unchained* 14).

Shadow Tricks (Ex): The teisatsu gains a single ninja trick (but not a master trick) of his choice. He cannot select a rogue talent in place of a ninja trick in this manner. If he selects a ninja trick marked with an asterisk (*), that talent applies to his hidden strikes instead of to sneak attacks, and the talent counts as a stalker vigilante talent with an asterisk (*) for the limitation of applying only one effect to a single hidden strike.

SOCIAL TALENTS

Vigilantes must always be prepared to use every possible trick and tactic to blend seamlessly into society, where they can hunt their prey from the cover of polite company. The following new social talents allow vigilantes on Golarion to act effectively in Golarion's many diverse political scenes.

Entrepreneur (Ex): Select any one Intelligence-, Wisdom-, or Charisma-based skill other than Perception or Use Magic Device. The vigilante can use the selected skill to earn money as if he were using a Profession skill. If he selects Perform or Profession, the vigilante instead gains the skill unlock powers for those skills as appropriate for his number of ranks in that skill (*Pathfinder RPG Pathfinder Unchained* 82). If he has the social grace[UI] social talent, he can apply this benefit to all skills selected with the social grace talent.

Guise of Life (Su): An undead vigilante with this talent gains an additional social identity in the form of one living creature identical to the vigilante's appearance in life. Successful Knowledge checks reveal information about the vigilante as if he were a living creature, and he counts as living for the purpose of divination spells and effects. He gains no other benefit from appearing to be a living creature, and remains vulnerable to positive energy and spells that effect undead. The vigilante must be a corporeal undead creature to select this talent. Humanoid vigilantes with the negative energy affinity racial trait can also select this talent, gaining a human social identity.

Guise of Unlife (Su): A vigilante with this talent gains an additional social identity in the form of an undead version of one of his existing social identities, such as a ghoul, vampire, or zombie. Successful Knowledge checks reveal information about the vigilante as if he were undead, and he counts as undead for the purpose of divination spells and effects. He gains no other benefit from appearing to be an undead creature, and remains vulnerable to negative energy and spells that effect the living. The vigilante must be a living creature to select this talent.

Well-Known Expert (Ex): The vigilante's social identity is known as an expert in numerous fields, including areas and topics the vigilante hasn't actually taken the time to study. As a result the vigilante is skilled at encouraging others to discover solutions to difficult problems themselves by asking probing questions, while appearing to give the information himself.

In his social identity, the vigilante can take 10 when attempting to aid another on Appraise, Craft, and Knowledge checks. He also gains a bonus equal to half his class level (minimum +1) on Bluff checks to appear knowledgeable in Appraise, Craft (all), and Knowledge (all). If he has the renown[UI] social talent, he grants a +3 bonus when he successfully aids another on these skill checks, rather than +2.

In his area of renown, the vigilante's social identity is so trusted as an expert that scholars are inspired to make amazing deductions and intuitive leaps in discussions with him. A creature that has already failed a Knowledge check on a specific subject can attempt one additional check to gain information on the same topic if it receives an aid another bonus from the vigilante when doing so.

Intrigue Feats (Ex): The vigilante gains one of the following feats as a bonus feat: Blustering Bluff[UI], But a Scratch[UI], Call Truce[UI], Confabulist[UI], Criminal Reputation[UI], Cutting Humiliation[UI], Esoteric Linguistics[ACG], Intoxicating Flattery[UI], Ironclad Logic[UI], Nerve-Racking Negotiator[UI], Orator[ACG], Persuasive Bribery[UI], Play to the Crowd[UI], Quick Favor[UI], Rhetorical Flourish[UC], Sense Assumptions[UI], Sense Relationships[UI], or Street Smarts[UI]. He must meet the feat's prerequisites. This talent can be selected multiple times; each time, the vigilante gains a new feat from the above list.

VIGILANTE TALENTS

Combining guile and an intimidating presence, each vigilante has a unique method of capturing and dispatching his marks once he has located them.

Concealed Strike (Ex): Whenever the vigilante attacks an opponent with a concealed weapon that his target wasn't aware of, he can attempt a Bluff check to feint that opponent as a move action. If he has the Improved Feint feat, he attempts this check as a free action instead. A vigilante must be at least 6th level to select this talent.

Fantastic Stride (Ex): The vigilante gains Spring Attack as a bonus feat, ignoring its prerequisites. At 10th level and every 4 levels thereafter, the vigilante can designate one additional creature when he uses Spring Attack.

The vigilante's movement this round does not provoke attacks of opportunity from any of these secondary creatures. A vigilante must be at least 6th level to select this talent.

Major Magic (Sp): A vigilante with this talent gains the ability to cast a 1st-level spell drawn from the same spell list as the minor magic talent. The vigilante can cast this spell once per day as a spell-like ability for every 4 vigilante levels he has. The caster level for this ability is equal to the vigilante's level. The save DC for this spell is equal to 10 + the vigilante's Intelligence modifier (for psychic, sorcerer/wizard, and witch spells), Wisdom (for cleric, druid, and shaman spells), or Charisma (for bard spells). A vigilante must be at least 4th level, have the minor magic vigilante talent, and have a score of at least 11 in the appropriate ability to select this talent.

Minor Magic (Sp): A vigilante with this talent selects one of the following spells lists: bard, cleric, druid, psychic, shaman, sorcerer/wizard, or witch. Once this decision is made, the selection cannot be changed. The vigilante gains the ability to cast a 0-level spell from the selected spell list. This spell can be cast two times per day as a spell-like ability. The caster level for this ability is equal to the vigilante's level. The save DC for this spell is equal to 10 + the vigilante's Intelligence modifier (for psychic, sorcerer/wizard, and witch spells), Wisdom (for cleric, druid, and shaman spells), or Charisma (for bard spells).

Mockery (Ex): The vigilante gains Antagonize[UM] as a bonus feat. He can target a creature with the Intimidate version of Antagonize twice each day, rather than just once. At 12th level, the effects of the Intimidate version of Antagonize last a number of rounds equal to the vigilante's Charisma modifier (minimum 1).

Team Player (Ex): The vigilante gains Swift Aid[APG] as a bonus feat, ignoring its prerequisites. Additionally, the vigilante can choose to use the feat as a standard action, in which case it applies to every ally adjacent to the vigilante. At 10th level, he can increase the bonus provided to one ally by this feat to +2 by using the aid another action as a move action rather than a swift action.

Take 'Em Alive (Ex): The vigilante doesn't take the usual –4 penalty on attack rolls made to deal nonlethal damage with weapons that normally deal lethal damage. In addition, the vigilante gains a +1 bonus on all attack and damage rolls for attacks that deal only nonlethal damage and have no secondary effects (such as poison). This bonus increases by 1 at 5th level and every 3 levels thereafter, to a maximum of +5 at 20th level.

Espionage Spells

From the ninja clans of Minkai to Taldor's Guild of Silence, spies across Golarion rely on magical means to follow targets and infiltrate social events in order to gather the intelligence their organizations require to further their aims. The following spells allow cunning spellcasters to distract enemies and steal their secrets without anyone being any wiser.

CLAIM IDENTITY

School transmutation (polymorph); **Level** alchemist 3, antipaladin 3, bard 3, druid 4, inquisitor 3, shaman 4, sorcerer/wizard 4, witch 3

Casting Time 1 standard action

Components V, S, M (a needle and thread)

Range touch

Target humanoid creature touched

Duration 1 hour/level

Saving Throw Fortitude negates; **Spell Resistance** yes

You steal the target's face, transforming yourself into a flawless imitation of it. All of the target's facial features, vocal cues, and identifying physical traits change, transforming it into an unremarkable member of its race and gender. You transform into a perfect likeness of the target's true form, as if affected by *alter self*, and gain a +10 bonus on Disguise checks to impersonate the original subject of this spell; you take no penalties on this check if the original target is of a different race, age, size, or gender.

Claim identity prevents any other polymorph effects from restoring the target's true face for the spell's duration, though the target can still assume other forms or faces via magic or any natural shapechanging ability.

CLAIM IDENTITY, GREATER

School transmutation (polymorph); **Level** alchemist 5, antipaladin 4, bard 5, druid 6, inquisitor 5, shaman 6, sorcerer/wizard 6, witch 5

Casting Time 1 standard action

Components V, S, M (a silver needle costing 100 gp)

Range touch

Target humanoid creature touched

Duration 1 hour/level

Saving Throw Fortitude negates; **Spell Resistance** yes

This spell functions as per *claim identity*, except it transforms its target into a helpless, inanimate porcelain mask for the spell's duration. The target remains aware of everything it can see or hear while transformed. The target can't speak or move, but can still take purely mental actions (such as casting certain spells) or be targeted by spells that affect its mind.

Any creature donning this mask is transformed into a flawless imitation of the spell's target, as if affected by *claim identity*, and reverts to its natural form upon removing the mask. Any damage dealt to the mask immediately ends this spell.

EGORIAN DIPLOMACY

School enchantment (compulsion) [mind-affecting]; **Level** bard 1, cleric 1, inquisitor 1, magus 1, mesmerist 1, psychic 1

Casting Time 1 standard action

Components V, S, M (a bent coin)

Range close (25 ft. + 5 ft./2 levels)

Target one creature

Duration instant; see text

Saving Throw Will negates; **Spell Resistance** yes

As part of casting this spell, you can attempt a single Intimidate skill check to make a target act friendly toward you. If you succeed, the target assists you normally, but *Egorian diplomacy* clouds the memory of any threats or pressure you applied. The target remembers assisting you, but can't remember why, and its attitude toward you doesn't worsen as a result of being intimidated.

Whether a creature fails or succeeds at its saving throw, it becomes immune to further castings of *Egorian diplomacy* for 24 hours.

GARRULOUS GRIN

School necromancy [fear, mind affecting]; **Level** antipaladin 2, bard 2, inquisitor 2, mesmerist 2, psychic 2, shaman 2, spiritualist 2, witch 3

Casting Time 1 round

Components S

Range close (25 ft. + 5 ft./2 levels)

Target one creature

Duration 1 hour/level (D)

Saving Throw Will negates; **Spell Resistance** yes

This Nidalese spell plants a seed of supernatural fear deep in a subject's mind, causing self-doubt, stuttering, and evasiveness. Affected creatures have difficulty meeting anyone's gaze and seem dishonest or guilty. The target takes a –4 penalty on Bluff and Diplomacy checks to convince another of the truth of her words, and on Diplomacy or Intimidate checks to influence another creature's attitude.

INSECT SCOUTS

School divination; **Level** antipaladin 4, bard 4, druid 2, inquisitor 3, psychic 4, ranger 2, shaman 2, sorcerer/ wizard 3, summoner 3, witch 3

Casting Time 1 round

Components S, M (a drop of honey)

Range close (25 ft. + 5 ft./2 levels)

Effect one insect scout/4 levels

Duration 1d6 hours, plus 1 hour/level; see text

Saving Throw none; **Spell Resistance** no

A favorite in the creaking courts of Ustalav, *insect scouts* summons one or more vermin to investigate a single location or building you can see. Your scouts must spend 1d6 hours investigating the target location, but need no oversight. When done, they return unerringly to you with their findings, traveling up to 1 mile per caster level you have to rejoin their master. Each insect's size is Fine. Each insect has 1 hit point, AC 20 (+2 Dexterity, +8 size), a movement speed of 5 feet, a climb speed of 5 feet, and a fly speed of 20 feet (perfect maneuverability). The insects use your saving throw bonuses, have a total Perception skill bonus equal to 5 + 1/2 your caster level, and can't attack. Because of their incredibly small size and magical nature, they can attempt Stealth checks to avoid being noticed even if they lack a source of cover or concealment, and they have a total Stealth skill bonus equal to 18 + 1/2 your caster level.

Each scout that returns passes along memories of specific structural flaws, defenses, and alarms, granting you the ability to reroll one failed skill check per scout, as long as the skill check involves that specific location's layout, such as a Stealth check to sneak in, a Disable Device check to silence an alarm, or a Perception check to notice a trap. If even one scout returns, you also gain a rough understanding of the building's layout (at least, any portions your scouts could access). All insight (and the associated rerolls) fades 1 hour per caster level you have after the scouts return. Your insects remember nothing about creatures, and so provide no information about guardians or any conversations they may overhear.

PASSING FANCY

School enchantment (compulsion) [mind-affecting]; **Level** bard 2, mesmerist 2, psychic 2, sorcerer/wizard 2, witch 2

Casting Time 1 standard action

Components V, S

Range close (25 ft. + 5 ft./2 levels)

Target one living creature

Duration 4d4 rounds (D)

Saving Throw Will negates; **Spell Resistance** yes

Taldor's infamous Lion Blades imported this spell from the ninja clans of Minkai, and both groups use it to great effect when maneuvering among the shallow upper classes. When you cast the spell, you dictate one specific topic or recent event and instill a magical obsession with that subject within the target. An affected creature becomes fascinated by the topic, and becomes completely focused on discussing the event with anyone nearby, possibly wandering off or distracting unaffected creatures. *Passing fancy* has no effect on a creature with an Intelligence of 2 or less.

Because the target talks and interacts with its usual cadence, onlookers take a –10 penalty on Sense Motive checks to notice that anything is amiss with the target's behavior.

PASSING FANCY, MASS

School enchantment (compulsion) [mind-affecting]; **Level** bard 4, mesmerist 4, psychic 5, sorcerer/wizard 5, witch 5

Target one living creature/level, no two of which can be more than 30 ft. apart

This spell functions as per *passing fancy* except as noted above.

SCRIBE'S BINDING

School transmutation (polymorph); **Level** occultist 6, sorcerer/ wizard 9, witch 9

Casting Time 1 standard action

Components V, S, F (a book bound in precious metals and treated with rare oils, worth 1,000 gp per HD of the target)

Range close (25 ft. + 5 ft./2 levels)

Target creature touched

Duration permanent

Saving Throw Fortitude negates; **Spell Resistance** yes

Hermea's benevolent Council of Enlightenment uses this spell to humanely preserve their society's greatest minds from the ravages of time, though it has seen far more sinister employment when put to use by other organizations that have since discovered its utility. This spell binds a single creature into a prepared book, sustaining it in suspended animation and filling the book with its experience and knowledge. The tome weighs 10 pounds and has one page for every day of the subject's life. The cover and binding transform to reflect the subject's appearance, interests, and tastes. Every thought and memory—including those the target may have forgotten long ago—are perfectly transcribed within the enchanted pages, penned in excruciating detail in the language that the creature was thinking or speaking in when the event occurred. If a memory includes dialogue in a language the subject didn't understand, that dialogue is reproduced phonetically, and must be translated by a reader who knows that language. Any alterations to a subject's memories—such as by a *modify memory* spell—appear in a subtly different script; a successful DC 35 Linguistics check is needed to identify this.

Spells that modify or remove text—such as *erase* or *secret page*—also affect the target's memory if they persist after its release. *Modify memory* can be used to repair any changes to its original state, or alter the accounts recorded within the book. A creature imprisoned by *scribe's binding* automatically fails any saving throws against effects to change or modify its memories.

A target bound by this spell can be freed by only *freedom*, *miracle*, or *wish*. *Polymorph any object* restores the target's normal form for 24 hours. *Scribe's binding* makes the imprisoning tome supernaturally durable (hardness 20, 10 hp per HD the imprisoned creature had). Destroying the tome immediately slays the creature imprisoned within.

Magic Tools of the Trade

Whether they lurk within shadows or hide in plain sight, those who partake in espionage and infiltration need equipment that won't betray their presence. The following items are designed to accompany ninja, rogues, spies, and vigilantes in places where magic items are best left unseen.

MAGIC WEAPON SPECIAL ABILITIES

Undercover agents find the following magic weapon special abilities quite useful in the field.

CONCEALED	PRICE +7,500 GP
AURA moderate transmutation	**CL** 10th

This special ability can be placed only on a light or one-handed melee weapon. A *concealed* weapon alters its shape at its wielder's command, transforming into a non-weapon object of the wielder's choice. This object must be a mundane item whose size and shape is similar to that of the concealed weapon or smaller, and it must be sized for a creature of the same size as the weapon's intended wielder. For example, a Medium short sword can transform into a quill sized for a Medium creature, but it cannot transform into a saw sized for a Small creature. A *concealed* weapon cannot transform into a consumable item, and if its alternate form is that of a container, any contents stored within the *concealed* weapon's alternate form are ejected into the wielder's space when the weapon transforms back to its original form.

While transformed, a *concealed* weapon doesn't register as magical, as per *magic aura*, though it retains the weight, hit points, and any hardness of its original form. A *concealed* weapon cannot assume the form of an object made from a special material (such as adamantine) unless it is already made of that material. For instance, a wooden club cannot transform into a mithral frying pan, but a mithral dagger can.

Transforming a *concealed* weapon into a mundane form requires a standard action, while returning it to its weapon form requires a move action. This transformation lasts until it is changed back into its original form or has been left unattended for 8 hours, whichever comes sooner.

CONSTRUCTION REQUIREMENTS	COST +3,750 GP

Craft Magic Arms and Armor, *major creation*

CONCEALED, LESSER	PRICE +3,000 GP
AURA faint transmutation	**CL** 5th

This special ability can be placed on only light or one-handed melee weapons. A *lesser concealed* weapon functions as a *concealed* weapon (above), but can transform into only a mundane object of the same size and general shape of the weapon (determined at the weapon's creation). A melee weapon cannot have both this special ability and the *concealed* special ability.

CONSTRUCTION REQUIREMENTS	COST +1,500 GP

Craft Magic Arms and Armor, *major creation*

DEBILITATING	PRICE +1 bonus
AURA moderate necromancy	**CL** 7th

A *debilitating* weapon has wicked ridges and gleams maliciously in any amount of light. Whenever a *debilitating* weapon is used to attack an opponent that is denied its Dexterity bonus to AC and hits, that opponent takes a –1 penalty on attack rolls or to its AC for 1 round (wielder's choice). Any creature that is immune to sneak attacks is immune to this penalty, and any item or ability that protects a creature from critical hits also protects a creature from the penalties imposed by a *debilitating* weapon. Multiple hits from multiple *debilitating* weapons in the same round do not increase the penalty or its duration.

If the wielder has the debilitating injury (*Pathfinder RPG Pathfinder Unchained* 22) class ability, this special ability increases the penalty applied by the bewildered or disoriented effects by 1.

CONSTRUCTION REQUIREMENTS	COST +1 bonus

Craft Magic Arms and Armor, *bestow curse*, creator must have 5 ranks in Heal

SPECIFIC MAGIC WEAPONS

The items below are based on some of the new clandestine weapons introduced in *Pathfinder RPG Ultimate Intrigue*.

BITING BRACELET	PRICE 5,000 GP	
SLOT none	**CL** 10th	**WEIGHT** 2 lbs.
AURA moderate illusion		

This *+1 heavy wrist launcher*[UI] appears to be a lavish, gold bracelet. This functions like the *glamered* weapon special ability (*Pathfinder RPG Ultimate Equipment* 142), except a *biting bracelet* is able to only assume this one specific form, and can revert to its innocuous appearance 1 round after being used as a weapon.

CONSTRUCTION REQUIREMENTS	COST 2,775 GP

Craft Magic Arms and Armor, *disguise*, *magic aura*

GRAFTING BLADE	PRICE 4,370 GP	
SLOT none	**CL** 3rd	**WEIGHT** 1 lb.
AURA faint transmutation		

This plain-looking *+1 spring blade*[UI] is attached to a weather-beaten cedar grip. By speaking a command word, the wielder can magically merge the grip into a larger wood handle, such as a cane, club, staff, stylus, or oar, transforming the infused item into either a *+1 shortspear*, *+1 spear*, or *+1 siangham* (depending on the handle's size). The blade can even be affixed to magic items such as staves, rods, and wands so long as they are made of wood, but doing so renders their other magical properties nonfunctional until the *grafting blade* is removed.

Removing a *grafting blade* from an item it has merged with requires a full-round action, and leaves both items unharmed.

CONSTRUCTION REQUIREMENTS	COST 2,370 GP

Craft Magic Arms and Armor, *wood shape*

STIRGE LANCET

	PRICE 8,500 GP
SLOT none	**CL** 7th	**WEIGHT** —
AURA moderate transmutation		

This +1 returning featherweight dart[UI] transforms into an insect-sized stirge when fired. As with a normal featherweight dart, a stirge lancet deals no damage; it instead administers 1 dose of an applied poison so long as the target doesn't have damage reduction, hardness, or similar abilities. If no poison is applied to the stirge lancet, it instead attaches to the target for 1 round and draws 1 ounce of blood or an equivalent fluid (if any) from the target. After applying poison or drawing blood, the dart flies through the air back to the creature that fired it. Unlike other featherweight darts, a stirge lancet is not damaged or destroyed when used, and can be reused indefinitely (though it can store only 1 dose of poison or one blood sample at a time).

Although a stirge lancet leaves no evidence, the sound of its buzzing wings may attract attention. A creature hit by a stirge lancet can attempt a Perception check to hear its humming; the DC for this check is equal to 20 + the stirge lancet's enhancement bonus on attack rolls (DC 21 for a standard stirge lancet). If the target succeeds at this Perception check, it instinctively attempts to bat the dart out of the air without a second thought, thinking the projectile to be an ordinary insect. There is a 50% chance that a dart so detected is batted from the sky, preventing it from returning to the creature that fired it and allowing it to be detected with a successful DC 15 Perception check, as normal for a featherweight dart. A batted dart is not destroyed, but must be retrieved manually.

CONSTRUCTION REQUIREMENTS	**COST** 4,400 GP

Craft Magic Arms and Armor, animate object, returning weapon[UC]

WONDROUS ITEMS

Those who operate in purposeful obscurity also require tools other than weapons.

MASK OF ANONYMOUS MIEN

	PRICE 25,000 GP
SLOT head	**CL** 10th	**WEIGHT** 1 lb.
AURA moderate transmutation		

This featureless mask is little more than a white disk with eyeholes and a pair of short leather straps for tying. After donning the mask, the wearer can meditate for 1 minute in order to assume a faceless identity, becoming an utterly generic and unremarkable member of the wearer's race and gender. Knowledge checks about the wearer's faceless identity don't reveal information about his true identity, unless his true identity is revealed to the world at large. Additionally, attempts to scry or otherwise locate the wearer work only if the creature is attempting to locate the wearer's faceless identity (or the creature knows the wearer's faceless identity and the wearer's true identity are one and the same). Otherwise, the spell has no effect, revealing nothing but darkness, as if the target were invalid or did not exist. In addition, if the wearer owns multiple masks of anonymous mien, the faceless identity he assumes is the same for all such items.

A vigilante who wears a mask of anonymous mien treats the faceless identity created by the item as a vigilante identity for the purpose of his class abilities, although this identity is separate from his actual vigilante identity.

CONSTRUCTION REQUIREMENTS	**COST** 12,500 GP

Craft Wondrous Item, alter self, nondetection

TORC OF INNOCUOUS GEMS

	PRICE 1,800 GP
SLOT neck	**CL** 9th	**WEIGHT** —
AURA moderate illusion		

This simple platinum necklace has five sockets for gems. An ioun stone placed in a socket registers as nonmagical, as per magic aura, and confers no benefit upon the wearer. With a command word, the wearer can release all ioun stones held within the necklace, sending them into orbit around her head and gaining their full benefits.

CONSTRUCTION REQUIREMENTS	**COST** 900 GP

Craft Wondrous Item, magic aura

Next Month

For untold millennia, the humanoid races have dwelt alongside mighty wyrms. *Pathfinder Player Companion: Legacy of Dragons* explores the ripples left by a dragon's actions in the world. Learn to think, move, and fight like these legendary beasts, and call out the untapped potential in your own blood. Dragons stop being monsters and become your first step toward personal glory with *Legacy of Dragons*!

WOULD YOU LIKE TO KNOW MORE?

For a true spymaster, there are never too many secrets to learn! Supplement your character's arsenal of espionage options with the knowledge presented in these products.

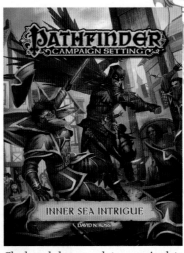

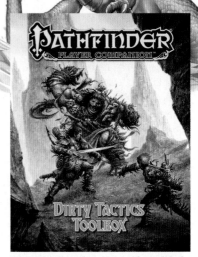

Whether you're taming the blood-soaked back alleys of your favorite metropolis or jockeying for the queen's favor alongside highborn nobles, *Pathfinder RPG Ultimate Intrigue* is an invaluable resource for any spymaster!

Cloak-and-dagger plots manipulate fates across the Inner Sea region. With *Pathfinder Campaign Setting: Inner Sea Intrigue*, you'll learn the many dangerous secrets hidden beneath the surface of the world of Pathfinder.

Embrace the subversive with *Pathfinder Player Companion: Dirty Tactics Toolbox*, a player-focused manual filled with loads of deliciously devious tips, tricks, and rules options to ensure that your character never has to face a fair fight.